CAMPFIRE STORIES
THE ADIRONDACKS

CAMPFIRE STORIES

THE ADIRONDACKS

TALES & TRAVEL COMPANION

edited by
ILYSSA KYU & DAVE KYU

For our little barnacle and seal, Lula and Isla.
We'll always be your rock.

MOUNTAINEERS BOOKS is dedicated to the exploration, preservation, and enjoyment of outdoor and wilderness areas.

1001 SW Klickitat Way, Suite 201, Seattle, WA 98134
800-553-4453, www.mountaineersbooks.org

Copyright © 2025 by Ilyssa Kyu and Dave Kyu

All contributors to *Campfire Stories: The Adirondacks* retain the copyright to their work.

All rights reserved. No part of this book may be reproduced or utilized in any form, or by any electronic, mechanical, or other means, without the prior written permission of the publisher.

Mountaineers Books and its colophon are registered trademarks of The Mountaineers organization.

Printed in China

28 27 26 25   1 2 3 4 5

Design and layout: Melissa McFeeters

Library of Congress Cataloging-in-Publication data is on file for this title at https://lccn.loc.gov/2024948046

Mountaineers Books titles may be purchased for corporate, educational, or other promotional sales, and our authors are available for a wide range of events. For information on special discounts or booking an author, contact our customer service at 800-553-4453 or mbooks@mountaineersbooks.org.

Printed on FSC®-certified materials

ISBN (paperback): 978-1-68051-748-4
ISBN (ebook): 978-1-68051-749-1

An independent nonprofit publisher since 1960

Contents

7   Introduction: Healing in a Second-Chance Wilderness

17   Storytelling Tips

ADIRONDACK STORIES

22   "In the Adirondacks" by Matt Dallos

39   "Shanty Days" by Jeanne Robert Foster

42   "State Land" by Jeanne Robert Foster

45   "The Wilderness" by William H. H. Murray

51   "Blue Line Medicine" by Robin Wall Kimmerer

58   "After Finding a Photo of Kensett's *Lake George, 1858* in the Paper" by June Frankland Baker

61   "Woodswoman" by Anne LaBastille

74   "Maple Sugar Moon" by Joseph Bruchac

81   "The Blanket Tree" by Joseph Bruchac

92   "The Lower Saranac" by Alfred B. Street

94   "My Canoe" by Alfred B. Street

97   "Time by the Lake" by William Chapman White

101   "How the Birds Got Their Feathers" by David Fadden

109   "Blinded by the Light" by Elizabeth Folwell

115   "Loon Calls" by Alan Steinberg

118   "Fish Stories" by Henry Abbott

126   "Wandering Home" by Bill McKibben

EXPLORE THE ADIRONDACKS

136   Map

138   What to Do

148   How to Visit Well

153   Towns to Visit

155   Where to Camp

157   Community Resources

162   Essential Reads

164   Acknowledgments

167   Permissions and Sources

171   Directory

176   About the Contributors

INTRODUCTION

Healing in a Second-Chance Wilderness

WHEN WE FIRST ARRIVED in the Adirondacks, our understanding of the place was ... limited. We live about a six-hour drive from the area, not a short distance by any means but certainly closer than our annual pilgrimage to Maine. We were *aware* of its existence and its woodsy mystique—our minds conjuring up lushly forested mountains, lakes, birch bark, sloping wooden chairs, family homes, and summer camps—but beyond that, the Adirondacks were a bit of a mystery.

We arrived at Lake George late one evening in early fall. Stepping out of the car in near total darkness at the off-season resort—a nicely appointed motel on prime lakeshore real estate—we began to understand how this place can take hold of you from the first inhalation of North Country air. We couldn't see the thirty-two-mile-long lake just down the slope from the parking lot, but we could *feel* its presence. It didn't take long for us to realize "the Adirondacks" isn't just a *place*, but a feeling, a state of mind, a full sensory experience that in an instant reminds you of the sheer pleasure of being alive on this planet.

The next morning we drove around—breathing the crisp air, and feeling a fire of optimism stirred up by the radiant reds and oranges of East Coast foliage. Knowing we were here for book research and the days ahead would be filled with interviews, museum visits, and scouring library shelves to find authentic local stories, we savored these moments. At times, driving down a country road made us feel as though we could be swallowed by the trees. We were certain some of the distant forests looked exactly how they had hundreds of years ago—ancient, lush, undisturbed. Then, just like that, we were navigating the throes of fast food joints and gas station convenience stores—things we were hoping to escape, yet handy when we realized how woefully understocked our snack stash was.

It was not lost on us how magical and charming these towns were, nestled among mountains, lakes, and streams. We wondered how this could be, without the protection of national park status—until we learned much of the Adirondacks *had* been logged (or farmed) before, and that we *were* in a park. In fact, when you cross the Blue Line, you're standing in one of this country's greatest experiments, what some say is *the* greatest rewilding project in the US, a laboratory of sorts.

The stories in this volume will introduce you to the Adirondacks much more eloquently than we ever could, but this introduction would be incomplete if we failed to say the very first thing every Adirondacker wants you to know: the Adirondack Park is extremely special, with its own unique wildlife and ecosystems, and its own unique history, culture, and community. There really is no other place like it, and it's easy to be giddy with this insight once you know it.

At 6 million acres, the Adirondack Park is the largest publicly protected area in the contiguous United States, established by the New York state legislature in 1892 "to be forever reserved for the free use of all the people." This unusual state park, with wild lands and settlements, is also a National Historic Landmark, and 2.7 million acres are included in the New York Forest Preserve, designated in 1894 in the New York state constitution as "forever wild," ensuring its protection in perpetuity. This is not just a cute and aspirational motto, as we had first assumed. It is the reason the Adirondack Forest Preserve as we know it today exists.

This was once a land where mountain lions and moose ruled, but overharvesting in the nineteenth and twentieth centuries led to significant deforestation and destruction of its diverse ecosystems, wildlife habitat, and waterways. Strict laws essentially brought an end to the timber and lumber industries that ravaged the landscape—though there are still some timber holdings within the park—and since being formally protected, the Adirondacks have roared back to life. This "second-chance wilderness" now boasts a healthy 8,000 square miles of mountains, three thousand lakes and ponds, 1,500 miles of rivers, and 850,000 acres of wetlands—including bogs, fens, and deepwater marshes. Moose have even found their way back, and some believe mountain lions have, too.

Unlike our national parks—which at times feel like a Disney World of the outdoors with iconic entrance signs, cheery uniformed rangers, visitor centers, and facilities within defined borders—the Adirondack Park is a mix of public and private land. Nearly half of the park is owned by New York State; the rest is held by individual landowners, corporations and organizations, timber companies, and conservation easements, which allow private ownership, business, and residence, while prohibiting certain kinds of land use or development. Today, the Adirondacks boast 110 small towns within the park. All have functioning schools, banks, businesses, and services.

This great experiment wasn't the Adirondack Mountains' first. Timbuctoo, a name coined by abolitionist and Underground Railroad conductor John Brown, was a free Black settlement established in 1846 as a response to a law that denied Black men the right to vote unless they owned $250 in land or a home. Gerrit Smith—abolitionist, philanthropist, and social reformer—saw the opportunity to build a Black hamlet on forty acres of land in the Adirondacks that would offer an opportunity for three thousand settlers to be endowed with land and get to vote. However, without prior farming experience, knowledge of this difficult terrain, or the appropriate resources or equipment to successfully cultivate fertile crops, many families never came, and those who did left. Ultimately, only thirteen Black families lived in Timbuctoo between 1850 and 1870. While the experiment ultimately did not have the resources or support to succeed, it stands as a testament to the progressive spirit and a reminder of the unsung voices of this region.

Today, many people living in Adirondack communities acknowledge their lack of diversity and are making efforts to address it. The Adirondack Diversity Initiative was established in an effort to "make the Adirondacks a welcoming and inclusive place for both residents and visitors while ensuring a vital and sustainable Adirondack Park for future generations."

Many of the people we spoke to across the Adirondacks conveyed a rich and sometimes forgotten history of the many people and cultures who built the region. These include Jamaican agricultural workers; refugees and asylum seekers arriving through Canada; Japanese-American photographer Itsuzo Sumy, who chronicled life in Chestertown; and Solomon Northup, author of *Twelve Years a Slave*, who was born in the Adirondack Mountains. Among the many men who created and explored this park, their names forever enshrined as names of peaks, we discovered a

INTRODUCTION

local favorite, unsung hero Grace Hudowalski, the first woman to hike all forty-six major Adirondack peaks. "Amazing Grace" was a founding member of the Adirondack 46ers, organizing its first meeting and serving as its first president. She kept meticulous records that showed increased interest in the peaks, which later became an invaluable tool for advocating for their protection. To honor her legacy, the peak formerly known as East Dix—in the Dix Range, an entire range named for former New York Secretary of State John A. Dix—is now Grace Peak.

Notably, we felt the absence of Indigenous voices past and present in the area. In addition to reaching out to Indigenous tribes and visiting Indigenous-run museums and cultural centers, we typically seek Indigenous history and stories on the shelves of local libraries and archives, museums, and interpretive exhibits. All of these felt missing here.

Despite continually perpetuated myths that the Adirondack region was a vast uninhabited wilderness before it was a park, the area was (and still is) home to a number of Indigenous tribes. The Haudenosaunee ("People of the Longhouse") Confederacy, also known as the Iroquois Confederacy or Six Nations, includes the federally recognized Mohawk, Oneida, Onondaga, Cayuga, Seneca, and Tuscarora tribes. Formed as a way for the tribes to unite and create a peaceful means of decision making, the Haudenosaunee Confederacy may well be the oldest participatory democracy on earth. Much evidence suggests that the US Constitution was influenced by the Haudenosaunee Confederacy's constitution, which assigns equal roles to law, society, and nature.

Fortunately, we were able to connect with David Fadden, who runs the Six Nations Iroquois Cultural Center in Onchiota, founded by his grandfather, master storyteller Ray Fadden (Tehanetorens). We were first introduced to David through his artwork depicting the Iroquois creation story of Sky Woman at the Wells Memorial Library in Upper Jay. We were thrilled that David was enthusiastic to capture a story for our book that hadn't yet been written down, to further preserve and share Iroquois stories and culture in a region that sorely needs it.

Seeing opportunity in this resource-rich region, loggers, hunters, farmers, miners, trappers, and sawmill operators began arriving in the late 1700s, followed by settlers who were lured by the forest's healing properties and abundant opportunities to recreate. The wealthy families of the Gilded Age built sprawling "Great Camps," the sick came to heal in "cure cottages," and city folk came to escape the noise, congestion, and pace of daily life.

The Great Camps were where people of means came to experience this region's natural beauty in rustic luxury. They were grandiose plots of land and family compounds built by the wealthy elite—including the Rockefellers, the Vanderbilts, the Carnegies, and J. P. Morgan—typically along a lake and boasting multiple lodges, cabins, cottages, dining halls, and other buildings to support a lavish lifestyle. Their aesthetic inspired a style of architecture and interior design embracing the natural character of the Adirondacks by including native building materials like logs, stone, birch bark, and decorative branches. Today, the camps that are still standing have been designated as National Historic Landmarks, and some host summer camps, overnight lodging, guided hikes, and history tours. Recreation and relaxation are so core to the history and experience here that unique styles of watercraft and reclining chairs originated in these mountains.

The Adirondack landscape has long attracted seasonal residents, retirees, outdoor enthusiasts, and—much to our delight for this

INTRODUCTION

book—artists and writers who found in this landscape the solace, space, and inspiration to create. Today, the region is home to 132,000 year-round residents and 200,000 seasonal residents, many of whom live in villages—smaller than towns—or hamlets, tight-knit rural communities that, in size and population, are somewhere between a small cluster of houses and a village. These hamlets are scattered amidst forests and lakes, and provide a feeling of community and connection in remote areas.

We spoke to several "boomerang" residents who grew up in the Adirondacks and couldn't wait to leave, only to return as adults. They say that people come for the beauty but stay for the community—oh, and the six-million-acre wilderness playground out the back door. We spoke to Olivia Dwyer at the Adirondack Land Trust, who shared how she moved away to other mountain towns only to come back years later, realizing there's nowhere else with this kind of access to nature that doesn't require driving an hour or waking up at the crack of dawn to nab a parking spot. She said it's the type of place where traffic jams are caused by turkey flocks crossing the road, not crowds headed to ski slopes or hiking trails. For Olivia, this is a place where the firehouse is still the social center of a community, and she pays for a post office box just for the chance to socialize with people. Others we met through the Adirondacks Land Trust delighted in the fact that there's no *off-season* here, as each season offers new recreation activities and different ways of exploring the Adirondacks, and that each region has its own unique character. You can travel two hours and experience something completely different.

Another person we met mentioned that they had always hated winter before coming to live in the Adirondacks later in life, but found that the joy full-timers have for every season is infectious. Winter brings frozen lakes and the quiet, serene landscape made by snow. Spring, also called mud season or black fly season, can be a blissful time of new growth and warmer air when wildflowers grow and maples flow. Summer, though busy, provides opportunities for bike rides and dips in the lakes, though locals keep their favorite spots secret. Fall brings the changing colors and cool, crisp air that zaps the mosquitos, making for comfortable days spent outside.

The Adirondacks see anywhere from seven to ten million visitors a year. Many visit Lake Placid, host of both the 1932 and 1980 Winter Olympic Games. Most famously, the "Miracle on Ice" happened here—the US ice hockey team, largely considered underdogs, defeated the long-favored Soviet Union team to win the gold medal in the 1980 Winter Olympic Games. More than forty years later, sports fans come to Lake Placid to tour, or even play in, the Olympic sites and facilities, and to participate in winter outdoor activities like skiing and snowboarding.

In the warmer months, many people who visit the Adirondacks experience much of what drew people here since the late nineteenth century—ample opportunities for rest, relaxation, hiking, camping, fishing, and paddling. Many base their adventures from the well maintained and accessible state campgrounds here; these were some of the first facilities to embrace car camping. Campers can swim in lakes and rivers, or hop on a trail right from the campground.

Speaking of trails, a popular way to experience the Adirondack Park, and a big draw to this area, is hiking the High Peaks, the forty-six mountain peaks that crest at 4,000 feet or higher; the highest is Mount Marcy at 5,344 feet. These are challenging hikes, though many locals joke that the biggest challenge is finding a parking spot at the trailhead. We spoke to several residents who have climbed, or are working toward climbing, all forty-six peaks, including one of the youngest mountaineers to achieve this. She

INTRODUCTION

15

told us she did it because her mom sent her to outdoor groups as child care. Most everyone agreed that becoming an "Adirondack 46er" was *not* the quintessential way to experience the Adirondacks, however—it's the forests, lakes, and streams below the peaks that ought to be sipped and savored like a glass of fine wine.

You can easily miss the beauty in the details here if you don't slow down to look for them. When you're only focused on reaching a summit, you can't hear the song of a hermit thrush, the drip of a maple, the babble of a brook, the yodel of a loon, the rhythm of oars paddling by. We chose the short stories, personal essays, and poems collected here to capture a range of quintessential Adirondack experiences and perspectives, acknowledging the history and heritage of this place while also conveying some of the quieter sounds and forgotten voices of the Adirondack forest.

These stories are meant to be read around a "fire"—whether quietly to yourself from the comfort of your couch or aloud to the people sharing the ember glow of a campfire with you. These are not stories for those seeking just to be entertained, but instead are for all those who have a curiosity about how certain special regions came to be and why they continue to mean so much to us. The stories we chose for this book convey wisdom that we believe should be an integral part of wilderness preservation, guiding you through the unique Adirondack landscape using all of your senses—the scent of balsam, the sight of light bending around the trees, the taste of maple syrup, the sounds of water flowing over stone and loons calling as you paddle across lakes. The stories in this book usher you through the gifts each season brings. They teach us all lessons of resilience, mountain medicine, and the powers of the forest that healed us as it healed itself—leaving us with a hopeful message that we can repair past mistakes, see new ways forward, and become healers of the land.

To identify these themes and choose stories for this collection, we interviewed many individuals who live and work here. We spent many days inside libraries, archives, and bookstores, sneaking out to spend time in the Adirondack Mountains and its trails, peaks, lakeshores, streams, and forests, its rich natural and cultural landmarks. We sought recommendations and insights from locals and combined them with our own experiences to create a guide to visiting this beloved place—practical tips about where to go, what to do, and where to camp, as well as ideas for how to visit in ways that support the resident communities, both human and wild.

Whether you've been summering in the Adirondacks your whole life, are a full-time resident, or are visiting for the first time through the pages of this book, we hope this collection deepens your connection to this majestic and mystical place. Light a campfire or your birch bark candle and enjoy a little maple syrup in your coffee as you take a stroll through this "forever wild" place.

Storytelling Tips

Storytelling has always been a fundamental part of being human. Beyond entertainment, stories have allowed us to share knowledge, traditions, and ideas, and to feel a sense of connection with people and places beyond our own experiences for thousands of years.

Through all its forms, we have witnessed how stories can create deeper emotional connections between people and the natural world. This is especially true across generations and communities who have been disconnected from the outdoors, yet who are, increasingly, responsible for protecting it.

We believe that stories are best when they're shared with others, so we encourage you to share any stories or sections you love with friends or family, continuing in the tradition of oral storytelling, by sharing them aloud.

Should you find yourself gathered with others around a campfire, here are some tips for sharing a story:

Be prepared. A campfire can provide a warm, flickering light that sets the perfect mood but may not be adequate for reading a book, so bring a lantern, flashlight, headlamp, or book light. A glass of water can rescue you from a fit of coughing or a dry mouth, so keep it handy. In a camp setting with crickets and a crackling fire, you may be competing to be heard—sit or stand up straight, breathe from your diaphragm, and project your voice.

Choose the right story. Choose a story that matches your audience's interests, age, attention span, and the moment. Pay attention to length; if it's too long, consider summarizing and read aloud only a particularly interesting or engaging poem or passage.

Introduce the story. Explain why you want to read this story, what it's about, and who wrote it—keeping it short and sweet. (Feel free to use our insider knowledge from the "About This Story" sections to get your audience excited.) End with a thought about what you took away from it and a question to engage your listeners.

Bring the story alive. Every story, especially poetry, has its own rhythm. When you read aloud, read it slightly faster than you would naturally speak but without rushing. Keep your listeners' attention by breaking up the rhythm with a long pause or a different cadence. (But don't overuse this trick or overperform!) Be authentic, enunciate clearly, and let your natural reactions enhance the story without disrupting the flow.

Most of all, have fun! Whether reading this book around a campfire, in your living room, at a park, or tucked cozily in bed, we hope you will find something that makes the natural world come alive.

O gentle mountains—you who first arose
Above primeval waters in the West—
We honor you, as every campsite shows,
And love your ancient streams and rocks the best.
Time laid his hand on you so long ago,
That there are steeper crags than yours to scale,
But none, wherever mountain winds may blow,
With friendlier slopes, now smoothed by ice and gale.
We who have built our fires by your streams,
And climbed to view the sunrise from your peaks,
When we are far from you, the heart still dreams
Of the calm peace you bring to him who seeks.
Sweet Adirondacks, in our lonely hours,
Your pines are with us, and your mountain flowers.

—P.H.W. BACHMANN,
"ADIRONDACKS"

ADIRONDACK
STORIES

In the Adirondacks

MATT DALLOS

Excerpt from *In the Adirondacks: Dispatches from the Largest Park in the Lower 48*

To get there from any direction go up. Higher than the valleys all around, the Adirondacks is a place set apart. Where boreal plants venture south to meet temperate. Where the air is chill and the summer short. Where there's a home garden center called Zone 3, and a theme park called the North Pole. Where 1920s silent film directors shot Siberia, Alaska, and Switzerland. Up there, where the frontier held on until the twentieth century. Some people are convinced it still does and always will. Where one county the size of Rhode Island has zero traffic lights. Up there, where you can still see the stars. Where the breeze is balsam and pine. Where the sick went to take the fresh air cure. . . .

It's forest, mostly, and lakes and streams and marshes and swamps and bogs and fens and rivers where there's too much water for trees to grow.

There are mountains, too, rolling, billowing, peaked. But to call the Adirondacks the Adirondack Mountains is to ignore most of what's there.

Many millions of years ago the metamorphic bedrock of the Adirondacks began to rise. No one seems to know exactly why. Erosion tore into the bedrock dome. Glaciers plucked and grated, gouged and scraped. The bedrock—crumpled and contorted, all zigzags and curlicues—is a billion years old. Fifteen thousand years ago, the most recent glaciers began melting. They took their time. Silt, sand, pebbles, stones, cobbles, and boulders hung suspended in the stagnant ice, dribbled to the ground. I liked to stand on mountains with a good view and imagine boulders hitting bedrock in plinks and bangs. Before trees migrated back north, the Adirondacks was rubble.

All that rock, all that sand, it dammed creeks and rivers, a lake or wetland in every nook. Adirondack bedrock, mostly granite, some schist and gneiss, is impermeable. Every drop of rain and every drip of melting snow either runs off or puddles. If you could pick up the Adirondacks and tilt it, it would slosh. Rivers mingle swampy and then take the long way down, threads of dark water that bow and sweep and curl. Beavers, loggers, and industrialists built a bunch of dams, creating even more lakes that looked a lot like all the others. . . .

In 1892, New York state designated the Adirondack Park. Most people call it the Adirondacks, or the 'Dacks, or the Park. Some call it the A-D-K. At about six million acres, it's the largest park in the lower forty-eight. New Jersey, Vermont, and New Hampshire: each state is about the same size as the Adirondacks. Everyone who tries to make sense of its scale notes how multiple national parks could fit inside, arranged like a kindergartener's pasted collage. I'll repeat the calculus because even as a cliché it's astonishing: Glacier, Yellowstone; Grand Canyon, and the Everglades combined. Or Death Valley, Olympic, Yosemite, and the Great Smoky Mountains. You could live in the park for your entire life and still be a tourist on the other side. In the nineteenth century, Adirondack guides would only escort sportsmen through one region. When guides approached the boundaries of their local knowledge, they passed their clients on to someone else. Often I imagined it as much bigger than it really is. It would feel, roughly, the size of Alaska. Alaska is seventy times the size of the Adirondacks. It takes only two and a half hours to drive across the Adirondacks, a fact I try to ignore so I can dwell in my own inflated sense of scale.

It's a park, but not in the way we usually think about parks in the United States. Half is private, half is public.

On private land, there are houses, grocery stores, marinas, nursing homes, car dealerships, industrial zones, garbage dumps (where tourists used to gather on summer evenings to feed marshmallows to black bears, a spectacle I was, sadly, born a few decades too late to witness), strip malls main streets with rows of local shops, condominiums, camps—thousands and thousands of Adirondack camps: vacation homes available in all sizes, shapes, styles, and price points— playgrounds, theme parks, golf courses, and luxury resorts that boast Big City chefs. For the record, my disappointment in never witnessing black bears eating marshmallows is because I would've enjoyed seeing a bear bounce up and down on the hood of some tourists cherry 1965 Buick Riviera. Also, I should add, there are a few strip mines, hunting lodges, ice cream stands, neighborhoods, motels, hotels, and hospitals. There's one Walmart. . . .

· ✦ ·

Nearly all state land in the Adirondacks is Forever Wild: no trees may be killed or damaged, a protection embedded within the state's constitution since 1894. Forever Wild trees can't be logged, cut to build a shelter, or hacked down with a battery-powered chainsaw to cook vegetarian bacon on a frosty morning. Forever Wild places this half of the park among the best-protected environments in the nation. Some Forever Wild trees are a few hundred years old, and in a few hundred years many more will be. Forever Wild created a forest that's well on its way to being classified old growth.

That wasn't necessarily the plan. In the 1890s, cut-and-run loggers were shearing the Adirondack forest. Business owners feared this would cause downstate canals to run dry. Proponents of Forever Wild intended the rule to preserve the state-owned forest temporarily, so that in a few years the trees could be managed—that is, logged—according to the nascent principles of scientific forestry. Fearing corruption, desolation, drought, and inferno, wealthy landowners who loved the wild woods stopped that plan. With the rise of environmentalism in the twentieth century, Forever Wild took on new meaning: an untouched wilderness, an ethos some environmentalists like to believe the Adirondacks has always had.

Most Forever Wild trees still stand. But over the years New York has cut quite a few, to build campgrounds and roads and snowmobile trails and ski slopes and fire observation towers and a scenic highway to the rocky, wind-torn top of the fifth-highest peak. Environmentalists often sue. With the exception of rocks, lawsuits might be the most abundant crop in the Adirondacks. Is Forever Wild land a recreational playground or a business opportunity? A remote wilderness or a profitable woodlot? Forever Wild, that

Adirondack motto, seen on T-shirts, beer coozies, legal documents, and at least one license plate issued west of the Rocky Mountains: the problem is no one can quite agree on what it should mean. . . .

· ✦ ·

In the late eighteenth century, the state owned the whole region (after seizing it from the British who had stolen it from Native Americans). That wasteland up north—the state tried to give it all away. No one really wanted it. A few decades later, after realizing its blunder, the state wanted to buy it all back but balked at the now lofty price per acre. (One village is named Speculator.) Over the years, the state has purchased more and more land, parcel by parcel, but long ago gave up on a monopoly. I'm glad they gave up. The Adirondacks would be boring if it were all Forever Wild, if it lacked towns and citizens and motels with metal roofs faded to a dull fuchsia.

At least 130,000 people live in the Adirondacks. Six million acres: that gives each resident roughly forty-six acres of elbow room. That fact didn't strike me as significant until I realized that's half as much as each resident of Montana, a state I think of as being hopelessly expansive and lonely. (Alas, each resident of Alaska has 575 acres.) Most Adirondackers live on the eastern edge and many commute to jobs in small cities outside. Some live in isolated hamlets scattered in the forest like a throw of jacks. In those hamlets, there aren't many year-round jobs, and residents are either retired or work for the local government, work in tourism, or piece together a living somehow. One Adirondacker said he made a living in the 1870s by "guiding, hunting and fishing" and anything he "could turn his hand to in the woods." Which isn't that different from the way many residents in isolated hamlets get by today.

There are even more part-time Adirondackers, around 200,000. They own Adirondack camps as second homes and pay local property taxes but don't get to vote in local elections. At camp, they spend the summer, deer season, snowmobile season, or just a weekend or two. July and August, part-timers outnumber locals in many towns. To locals, how many years you've lived there full-time is a status symbol. It takes at least a decade of winters, mud seasons, and biting black flies before you're no longer a flatlander. Bicknell's thrushes are all Flatlanders, I'll always be one, too, and that lady behind the desk at the Red Top Inn knew it.

Here's what really sets the tone of the region: There are eight or ten or twelve million annual tourists. No one's quite sure. Unlike most national parks, there's no entrance gate, no smiling ranger with a badge and a wide-brimmed hat collecting thirty-five bucks and handing you a map. Almost 84 million people live within a day's drive. The Adirondacks is the Northeast's wilderness backyard. Has been for two centuries. Most tourists show up on the Fourth of July. Labor Day is The Exodus. Locals stand on the side of the road to wave goodbye. A tall tale, I thought, until I saw it for myself. Since the 1870s, when the Adirondacks first became a fashionable tourist destination, most people who have seen the Adirondacks have seen it green....

Back at the Red Top Inn I watched some television, read for a bit. White tractor trailers hauling woodchips roared by on the road every thirty minutes or so. I could hear them from a long way off, and I imagined those white tractor trailers barreling through a sodden, dark forest the size of New Jersey: headlights and taillights, splash and clang and a Doppler-effect rumble. This was a land of leisure and wilderness, I had thought, a place to be enjoyed, a place to escape the modern world. There I was sulking about brain drain and poverty and jobs and woodchips in white trucks while I stared at the glint of silver insulation in the uneven gaps between the rustic boards on three walls of Room #6. What was I doing up there? Why did I care about this region and its past and future? What was I looking for? These weren't just questions about me. They were about wilderness and culture and America, about the way we look at the land and how we're drawn to what's wild and what we think is unknown, and about what that means for how we value the world around us and what we choose to protect.

Trying to fall asleep on a flimsy mattress under a roof once red, I thought back to my history in this place. After college, my girl-friend, now wife, and I had spent a weekend up there each summer, camping, hiking, wandering souvenir shops. Two weekends if we were lucky. After the long drive up, Erin and I would park next to a lake and get out to gaze at pines and rocks in the fading light. We felt as though we had entered another realm. A loon would wail or a coyote would yap, as if the moment had been queued up for our arrival. We'd inhale the tangy balsam air and make big eyes at each other, awestruck by the scenery, the silence, the heft of so many trees. I remember feeling a giddy sense of wonder that this place existed, that it was open for the public to explore. I didn't yet know the history of the area. I didn't even consider that it had a history. It seemed it had always been and would always be a wilderness open to tourists. Open for tourists. I remember seeing a real estate ad that boasted about a camp that sat within six million acres of wilderness. A lark, clearly. Even back then Erin and I laughed it off. But it seemed to speak some truth about the way many flatlanders felt about the area. . . .

· ✦ ·

Over the past ten thousand years or so, this is what's happened in the Adirondacks:

Native Americans lived there. They still do and have since not long after the glaciers melted. The Haudenosaunee and Algonquian peoples and their predecessors traded, hunted deer and moose and maybe caribou, fished by wooden torch, sang, danced, died, gave birth, told stories, hunkered down out of the winter wind, slapped mosquitos and blackflies, chipped stones into points, grew corn and then ground it with stone pestles. I often wondered about their names for lakes and mountains. Rocks too. If the next nineteen pages of this book were filled with the unrecoverable traces of that time, it would more accurately display the scale of Indigenous Adirondack occupancy.

Europeans arrived on the fringes about four hundred years ago. To more accurately display the scale of European occupancy, that sentence would dangle, alone, at the end of those nineteen pages.

The Europeans purchased every beaver pelt they could. Various would-be colonizers dreamed it a virgin land of jewels and precious metals. The Dutch feared it might harbor unicorns. The first European to cross the Adirondacks, long before it was called that, was either an ambitious trapper or an abducted French missionary. Official maps depicted the region as a few rivers scattered on a blank spot. Native and European trappers scratched more accurate maps on birch bark....

Scientists, artists, and writers discovered the region. They wanted it to be a wilderness. So that's what they called it, and that's what most flatlanders have called it ever since. Scientists measured elevations and wanted to open it to progress, profit. Artists painted scenes: big rocks, shadowy pines, penumbral dusk light, and the luminous crescent of a sandy shore.

One geologist, Ebenezer Emmons, named the Adirondacks the Adirondacks in 1835. Emmons considered naming the Adirondacks Aganschioni because he thought Aganschioni had a better sound.

"Adirondacks" might have been a corruption of the name of a tribe that never lived or hunted anywhere in the Adirondacks. It might also have been an Anglicization of a derisive title the Haudenosaunee called some Algonquin tribes, meaning, possibly, bark eaters, because that's how those tribes survived famine, or because they dwelled in the forest, or because they cut fallen trees to clear a route down narrow rivers. It might have been a generic term for foreigners. Translation between languages might have confused the root for "tree" with the root for "rock," and the phrase might originally have been about a people who lived in the land of rock. That's the story I like best. Emmons intended for the name to apply to a single range of mountains. Later writers stretched it out. . . .

Two bald eagles land in a lightning-struck pine and fluff their feathers above the rocky point where I sit to watch sunset. The wind has died. Bald eagle feathers grating lightning scorched pine bark, that's all I can hear. It's wilderness reverie, an escape, a moment to reflect on the quiet places where we are fortunate enough to still find a scrap of calm that grants us peace. I recline on the still sun-warm shield of gray rock and tuck my hands behind my head, take in the view. Sunset blushes a neon pink beyond gray ridges, and when I trace the shapes of the ridges, which roll and dip and rise all across the panorama I can see, I think about the underside of the glacier that sculpted them, think about this landscape as the inverted form of the Ice Age, think about how all that ice pressed down and melted to leave this puddle hemmed in by rock and sand.

Then on the far shore I see it and it snaps me out of the myth. In some book I had read about it but had forgotten it would be there. Across the lake, in a break in the forest, there's a weedy clearing that was once a close-cropped lawn. The lawn once held a mansion, the wilderness retreat of a man who had married a Vanderbilt and then managed the construction of the only railroad to cross the Adirondacks, which opened the whole region up to tourists. In the living room there had stood a chimney of massive, rough-cut rocks, more crag than chimney. I've seen a photograph. A stuffed panther crouching on one ledge. Two stuffed bear cubs hiding in the nooks. Three bear rugs on the floor, and in the corner, on top of a cabinet, a stuffed fox standing alert. The panther might have been the last killed in the Adirondacks. It stood stuffed in a hotel, and then in someone's attic, and then William Seward Webb, the railroad man who owned the mansion, bought it.

How was I supposed to feel about this presence of the human past here in the wilderness? I tried to ignore it. By the time the pink had drained out of the sky and the eagles had moved on I had changed my mind, and I wished the state had let the chimney stand, those craggy blocks of stone where the stuffed carcass of what might have been the last Adirondack panther crouched, as a reminder of what this lake once was. I didn't have any particular affection for Webb's story, although I do appreciate that before he died he arranged to have a boulder from this property hauled to Woodlawn Cemetery in the Bronx as a footstone for his grave. There's a township named after him, and his story—rich man opening up the woods for more people to get there—is the type that Adirondack history tends to valorize. But I didn't want the land wiped clean. I wanted the chimney to be a ruin, a reminder of what it once was—a rich family's PRIVATE WATERFRONT, and before that the realm of a hunter and trapper who occasionally wore a cloak of furs, mangy and rank, and roamed down to the settlements to flaunt his collection of bird and animal skins, and before that a homeland of Native American tribes. I wanted to have land that could feel wild and still have a past we acknowledged. The state torched the mansion when it bought the land in 1979 and made it Forever Wild.

Forever Wild, that radical act of not cutting trees, is often viewed as a landmark victory in natural preservation, a turning point in the way we treat the land. If the Adirondacks appears in history textbooks, it's for that triumph. Forever Wild is framed as part of the inevitable progress we've made as a nation to take better care of the environment. But it also tends to cloak histories that don't match the escape from the world most of us think we want this place to be.

At dark the wind dies. I launch my canoe and float in a stillness that's a lapse in the progression of time....

To flatlanders the Adirondacks has long been a refuge from the outside world, a vacationland, a realm of repose, a place to get away from the everyday. Maybe [William H.H.] Murray deserves partial credit for starting it, his book establishing the Adirondacks as a healthful and adventurous but safe wilderness. But it preceded Murray. The Adirondacks sat there just north of an industrializing East Coast, waiting for us to realize we needed to flee the world we had built.

IN THE ADIRONDACKS

I felt it, too, this urge to escape, this idea that I should be enjoying myself up there. I started my travels for this book during the rancorous 2016 presidential election, and they continued through the Trump administration. I thought: here was an opportunity to recuperate, to rest, to look at the scenery for the sake of looking at the scenery. Crossing the Blue Line, I felt myself put the problems of the world behind me, as if a clunker of a kayak had just sailed off my car's roof and clonked down the road. *Lean against that pine. Enjoy the sun, the quiet, the clean air.* This sense of escape is why I spent so much time in my car driving. If I was driving, if I was on the move, I thought I wouldn't so easily fall for that Adirondack repose. I worried that if I went for a weeklong canoe trip, or if I backpacked into the most remote spot within the Blue Line, I'd lose any chance of maintaining distance from the myth. Driving, always getting back in my car and getting on the road, somehow gave me the distance I needed to achieve at least some perspective on this place and its myth, as if somehow I could outrun it if I never stayed in one spot for too long. This put me in a strange spot. I wasn't a tourist. I wasn't up there to relax, to get away. I wasn't a traveler passing through. I certainly wasn't a local going about my everyday routine. I was running from what I was also trying to chase.

Driving didn't always work, and I wonder if my inability to completely sever myself from the myth—in fact, at times my lack of interest in even trying to sever myself from the myth—skewed the places I visited and researched. If what I was doing up there was trying to assemble a biography of a place and an idea, did I overlook stories that could've offered important insights because they didn't fit what I thought the Adirondacks should be?

The abolitionist John Brown is buried in the Adirondacks, next to a big rock within view of the High Peaks. In 1849, Brown moved to the area to join a community of formerly enslaved people who had established an agricultural community. He never spent much time there, but that's where he chose to be buried after he was hung for his role at Harpers Ferry. Many times I drove within a few miles of his grave. I never visited. Why not? Did I think that story wasn't Adirondack enough? Did I think it was more important to go hike another High Peak? Was that the myth speaking? By not going to see Brown's grave, I had too easily accepted a static vision of the Adirondacks—as an escape from the everyday, as a region of wilderness removed from wider social concerns –rather than trying to imagine a vision of the Adirondacks that could be malleable over time, that could accommodate people and places that conflict with the myth, that could challenge it, that could question the way we think about the region.

What else gets overlooked? The Adirondack population is, on average, poor and aging. With retirees moving in and young people moving to the flatlands to find jobs—like those twentysomethings at the bar in Tupper Lake—many towns are struggling to staff volunteer fire departments and emergency services. Despite clean air and exceptional access to world-class outdoor recreation, many towns are seeing shrinking populations; some schools have closed or merged. Although overall the Adirondacks suffers from slightly less poverty than other rural counties with comparable demographics—primarily because of the boost from tourism— many of the available jobs are seasonal and low paying, with few opportunities for advancement, and pre-pandemic many of those positions went to guest workers visiting from other countries whom business owners could pay even less. There's drug addiction, just like everywhere else, of course. There's often stark income inequality between locals and flatlanders. There's a lack of local society. Older locals I talked to expressed nostalgia for thirty to forty years ago, when towns held more off-season gatherings and had frequent funky celebrations to get through mud season and the winter. Back then there was a sense of community, the feeling of a large family getting by in a remote land. Many towns now seem to be hemorrhaging the social vibrancy that's long made them a desirable place to live. A chain of gas stations with coffee shops has spread Blue Line to Blue Line over the past few decades, at least offering a year-round if not quite homegrown place for locals in many towns to gather. One afternoon, listening to NPR while I drove the long green blur, I caught a story about race in the Adirondacks. In the past few decades, much of rural America has begun to diversify. The Adirondacks has not. It's gradually becoming ever less diverse than many other areas of rural America. The radio story recounted a racist incident in an Adirondack bar: a White bouncer confronted a Black man with a blatantly racist comment and then two weeks later a White man at Walmart repeatedly hurled racist epithets at the same man. The story went on to relate the many violent ways, subtle and direct, that minorities face racism in the Adirondacks. It was a jarring realization for me. The entire region had always felt so open to me, free and safe to roam and explore. The radio story quoted a survey that had found 90 percent of visitors to the Adirondacks are White. Some of the most popular Wilderness Areas are in Hamilton County, a massive, roughly rectangular county that occupies the most remote portion of the central Adirondacks. According to a different survey, conducted in 2021 by an Adirondack tourism organization, 96 percent of flatlanders visiting Hamilton County identified as White or Caucasian; less than 1 percent identified as Black or African American.

The popular tale of the Adirondacks is a story about environmental protection, recreation, and escape. That's not good enough.

The problem with allowing such a narrow vision of a place to determine that place's story is that we crop that place's future.

The escape: If I close my eyes and think back to the first few times I drove up, I can recall the excitement of driving through Old Forge and feeling what I thought was wilderness all around me. I can feel what it was like to think of pines and boulders and silent ponds cascading into the distance and not think at all about local society or race or who cleaned the rooms at motels and whether or not their prevailing wage allowed them to feed their children fresh vegetables and buy a home with sufficient insulation for a night of −33, when, if anything, I went out of my way to avoid thinking about those issues. I could get away from the modern world, didn't have to worry about who had once lived on this land, or who lived there now, or who was excluded from enjoying time there. It was comforting to think that way because that's how most Americans have long thought about the outdoors. That's our heritage of the outdoors. The Adirondacks responds to that heritage, but it has also influenced it, even helped bolster it—might even be where it took root. If the Adirondacks is a geography that has influenced American thought about parks and wilderness and what it means to spend time there, I've realized I have to be open to the idea that influence of the Adirondacks has perpetuated or even introduced some ideas we need to change.

There are committed individuals and organizations fighting against these issues. They're making progress. But they operate within a narrative of the Adirondacks that works against them. To help, we need to find ways to think about this place that look beyond escape. If the Adirondacks has been a radical experiment in land preservation over the past century and a half, why can't it now become a radical experiment in the ways we begin to recognize that social issues are not separate from environmental

IN THE ADIRONDACKS   37

issues? Why can't it become a radical experiment of social and racial justice? Why can't the Adirondacks establish a model that can challenge the entire nation to reconsider the boundaries that exist for equal access to the outdoors? Why can't the Adirondacks become a place where we demonstrate how towns and villages and their social lives and economies should be an integral part of the way we think about wilderness preservation? Truly supporting the Adirondacks for the next century demands nothing less.

About This Story

In the Adirondacks: Dispatches from the Largest Park in the Lower 48 was recommended to us by the owner of The Bookstore Plus, a beloved bookshop in the Lake Placid community. Strolling the aisles of books with her reaffirmed the need for us to travel to these places and speak with locals, especially those familiar with the local literature and contemporary writers. An unassuming book by an author we weren't familiar with, it quickly became one of our favorites from the visit—if not *the* favorite. Editing down the selections from this book was agonizing—it's *that* good.

Typically we look for a piece that serves as an overview to kick off the story collection—one that provides context and grounds the reader in the unique landscape, history, and culture of a place. This piece, and the entire book for that matter, does exactly that and more. As Matt Dallos, a historian and ecological landscape designer, introduces us to the landscape and history of the Adirondacks, he also challenges us to look a little differently at the place and break down the mythology to explore its faults, its challenges, and the issues we ought to reckon with. Not only does this piece set the stage for this book, but we hope it also helps frame your point of view as you take in the stories that follow—including a story from the book by minister and early Adirondack camper William H. H. Murray that Dallos refers to as "establishing the Adirondacks as a healthful and adventurous but safe wilderness" and one by contemporary Indigenous storyteller David Fadden, whose tribe lived in harmony with the land for tens of thousands of years.

Shanty Days

JEANNE ROBERT FOSTER

It's hard to find the log roads in the woods
Or where they were; the shanty days arc gone,
But still I think the old days in the woods
Will be alive as long as one remembers them.
Sometimes its hard for me to figure out
Why no one talks about old shanty days
Except myself in these parts hereabout.

Maybe I've lived too long.... All men know now
When lumber's needed there's a power sawmill
They set up in a stand of spruce and pine.
There's hardly men alive who slept on bunks
In lumber shanties deep in the North Woods,
Choppers and limbers and the men who hauled the logs
Down to the river for the "run" in spring,
Or know a skidway, or how many "markets" cut,
Or why we peeled the hemlock bark in May.
If you speak up they only stare at you
And wonder where you've slept the years away.

My heart aches—for the lumbering days are gone
Though you may still find cuts in the deep woods,
If you remember where to look for them,
That led to big forgotten lumber jobs
With log shanties that bunked the men.

It was a clean hard life. Men went in when snow came
And didn't take the hay-road till the spring.
There were some farmers too who hired out
With regular lumberjacks when crops had failed
To earn a little cash to help the farm.
It was a great adventure when a boy
Went into the lumber-woods for the first time.
He had to earn his grub, to fight his way
Till the jacks saw he had the stuff it took
To hold his own and keep big bullies in their place.

We used to box and wrestle in the woods;
We stuffed our sheepskin leggings on our hands
For gloves and squared off in the long bunkhouse
After the grub. When I was sparring with Bob Smith
The men held up a broomstick just between
Our waists to teach us to stand up and box.
Bob swung too low, I biffed him on the nose.
I backed away and stumbled and went down
Upon a pile of wood beside the stove;
He came on fast and fell atop of me;
I was so young and scared I grabbed his waist
And hung on so he couldn't lift a mitt,
And then we laughed. We both were young and green,
And the old jacks dared us to fight again.

SHANTY DAYS

It was a good clean life—the crash of falling trees,
The smell of balsam and of spruce and pine,
The chittering of the jays, the skidways piled
With sappy logs, the resin on our hands,
The cook house with its pans of pork and beans
And johnny cake. . . . We had enough to eat.

The shanties—years have rotted them away,
Although you still can see where one has been
And what was once a clearing, by the logs
Of the foundation of the big bunk house.
I find them when I tramp old shanty roads,
Or what is left of them, grown up with brush.
Sometimes I sit down on a mossy stump
And shut my eyes. . . . The shanty days come back,
I hear the choppers axes on the trees,
The sound of limbing and the clank of chains
Hauling the logs down to the old skidway,
The shouts of "Timber!"—and I get the smell
Of slashed-down pine sweet with its resin sap.

It don't last long. I open up my eyes
And struggle back to what we call life now.

State Land

JEANNE ROBERT FOSTER

"Father, why did you make the timber lot
State land? If you must sell, why not to us?
Have you forgotten that your sons must live,
And timber's growing scarcer every day?
When the state took the mountainside we thought
That it would have no more. Now you have sold
Two hundred acres of fine timber land,
And we who follow you must go without
All that the land would bring in years to come,
With its rich stand of hemlock and of pine."

"I think, my sons, that you in time will see
My reasons; you are young and moving out
Upon the tide of what to me is strange.
You have new ways to struggle and to win,
More than I had, who cleared land for my farm.
I have watched spoilers come and take away
So much I hardly know my township here.
I gave the mountainside to keep it wild,
Free for the life that it has had so long.
The trail will always be what it is now.

STATE LAND

The summit, with its scrubby balsam trees,
A playground for the deer and porcupine.
The timberland—well, I walked over it
Before I gave the deed to join its soil
To our wilderness. Beyond my line
I looked down on the havoc of the years,
Dude ranches sprawling where farmhouses stood.
I have no quarrel with what you call 'our times,'
But my heart spoke: I must preserve this land.
I walked over the land from end to end;
Looked at the garnet outcrop, and the ledge
Of quartz where we found native amethyst,
And from the serpentine we used to carve into inkwells.

"I listened to the brook. The yellow
Lady-slipper grows there, and the pink,
And other flowers that fly the feet of men.
I touched the trees; somehow they sing to me;
The pine and hemlock leaning to the wind;
The birdseye maple and, where sun could touch,
The slippery elm we used for medicine.
There is a deadfall up there in those woods
They say the Indians built long, long ago.
It's rotted down, but you can see the way
The Indian hunters planned to catch a bear.
As I walked on I prayed this land might be
A sanctuary of our wilderness
That keeps the human soul close to its God.

"There are still two hundred acres of cleared land,
The beaver meadows, and the sugar bush and orchards

For my sons. In future years you will come here
And touch the trees as I have done,
And think that I did right."

About These Stories

Jeanne Robert Foster was born into poverty in the Adirondacks in 1879. She grew up in isolation among farmers and loggers, surrounded by Irish, Canadian, and French families who had fled famine in their home countries. *Adirondack Portraits: A Piece of Time* is a collection of Foster's writings that gives us a glimpse of the influence of her mother, a schoolteacher whose father was an abolitionist minister. Foster's mother "recognized the importance of education and pressed her daughter to study, to use her mind, and to look beyond the Adirondacks to a country in the midst of rapid growth, a country where exciting new adventures were opening up for women." Foster served as a model for artists and fashion designers, worked as a journalist in Boston and New York City, and traveled around Europe meeting world-renowned authors and artists.

The Adirondacks, though, were Foster's *home*, and she loved it fiercely despite its hardships. Her friend, Adirondack conservationist Paul Schaefer, wrote that "shining through her hardscrabble life . . . came the roar of majestic rivers, the sight of rainbows on high mountain cataracts and of deer bounding off through the dense woods, and the bewitching fragrance of a wilderness close at hand." We selected these poems for Foster's ability not only to capture the cultural heritage of the Adirondacks, but also to illustrate the tension between nostalgia and the practical realities of ensuring its preservation for future generations.

The Wilderness

WILLIAM H. H. MURRAY

Excerpt from *Adventures in the Wilderness*

The Adirondack Wilderness, or the "North Woods," as it is sometimes called, lies between the Lakes George and Champlain on the east, and the river St. Lawrence on the north and west. It reaches northward as far as the Canada line, and southward to Booneville. Its area is about that of the State of Connecticut. The southern part is known as the Brown Tract Region, with which the whole wilderness by some is confused, but with no more accuracy than any one county might be said to comprise an entire State. Indeed, "Brown's Tract" is the least interesting portion of the Adirondack region. It lacks the lofty mountain scenery, the intricate mesh-work of lakes, and the wild grandeur of the country to the north. It is the lowland district, comparatively tame and uninviting. Not until you reach the Racquette do you get a glimpse of the magnificent scenery which makes this wilderness to rival Switzerland. There, on the very ridge-board of the vast watershed which slopes northward to the St. Lawrence, eastward to the Hudson, and southward to the Mohawk, you can enter upon a voyage the like of which, it is safe to say, the world does not anywhere else furnish. For hundreds of miles I have boated up and down that wilderness, going ashore only to "carry" around a fall, or across some narrow ridge dividing the otherwise connected lakes. For weeks I have paddled my cedar shell in all directions, swinging northerly into the St. Regis chain, westward nearly to Potsdam, southerly to the Black River country, and from thence penetrated to that almost unvisited region, the "South Branch, without seeing a face but my guide's, and the entire circuit, it must be remembered, was through a wilderness yet to echo to the lumberman's axe. It is estimated that a thousand lakes, many yet unvisited, lie embedded in this vast forest of pine and hemlock. From the summit of a mountain, two years ago, I counted, as seen by my naked eye, forty-four lakes gleaming amid the depths of the wilderness like gems of purest ray amid the folds of emerald-colored velvet. Last summer I met a gentleman on the Racquette who had just received a letter from a brother in Switzerland, an artist by profession, in which he said, that, "having travelled over all Switzerland, and the Rhine and Rhone region, he had not met with scenery which, judged from a purely artistic point of view, combined so many beauties in connection with such grandeur as the lakes, mountains, and forest of the Adirondack region presented to the gazer's eye." And yet thousands are in Europe today as tourists who never gave a passing thought to this marvellous country lying as it were at their very doors.

Another reason why I visit the Adirondacks, and urge others to do so, is because I deem the excursion eminently adapted to restore impaired health. Indeed, it is marvellous what benefit physically is often derived from a trip of a few weeks to these woods. To such as are afflicted with that dire parent of ills, dyspepsia, or have lurking in their system consumptive tendencies, I most earnestly recommend a month's experience among the pines. The air which you there inhale is such as can be found only in high

THE WILDERNESS 47

mountainous regions, pure, rarefied, and bracing. The amount of venison steak a consumptive will consume after a week's residence in that appetizing atmosphere is a subject of daily and increasing wonder. I have known delicate ladies and fragile school-girls, to whom all food at home was distasteful and eating a pure matter of duty, average a gain of a pound per day for the round trip. This is no exaggeration, as some who will read these lines know. The spruce, hemlock, balsam, and pine, which largely compose this wilderness, yield upon the air, and especially at night, all their curative qualities. Many a night have aid down upon my bed of balsam-boughs and been lulled to sleep by the murmur of waters and the low sighing melody of the pines, while the air was laden with the mingled perfume of cedar, of balsam and the water-lily. Not a few, far advanced in that dread disease, consumption, have found in this wilderness renewal of life and health. I recall a young man, the son of wealthy parents in New York, who lay dying in that great city, attended as he was by the best skill that money could secure. A friend calling upon him one day chanced to speak of the Adirondacks, and that many had found help from a trip to their region. From that moment he pined for the woods. He insisted on what his family called "his insane idea," that the mountain air and the aroma of the forest would cure him. It was his daily request and entreaty that he might go. At last his parents consented, the more readily because the physicians assured them that their son's recovery was impossible, and his death a mere matter of time. They started with him for the north in search of life. When he arrived at the point where he was to meet his guide he was too reduced to walk. The guide seeing his condition refused to take him into the woods, fearing, as he plainly expressed it, that he would "die on his hands." At last another guide was prevailed upon to serve him, not so much for the money, as he afterwards told me, but because he pitied the young man, and felt that "one so near death as he was should be gratified even in his whims."

The boat was half filled with cedar, pine, and balsam boughs, and the young man, carried in the arms of his guide from the house, was laid at full length upon them. The camp utensils were put at one end, the guide seated himself at the other, and the little boat passed with the living and the dying down the lake, and was lost to the group watching them amid the islands to the south. This was in early June. The first week the guide carried the young man on his back over all the portages, lifting him in and out of the boat as he might a child. But the healing properties of the balsam and pine, which were his bed by day and night, began to exert their power. Awake or asleep, he inhaled their fragrance. Their pungent and healing odors penetrated his diseased and irritated lungs. The second day out his cough was less sharp and painful. At the end of the first week he could walk by leaning on the paddle. The second week he needed no support. The third week the cough ceased entirely. From that time he improved with wonderful rapidity. He "went in" the first of June, carried in the arms of his guide. . . . In five months he had gained sixty-five pounds of flesh, and flesh, too, "well packed on," as they say in the woods. Coming out he carried the boat over all portages; the very same over which a few months before the guide had carried him, and pulled as strong an oar as any amateur in the wilderness. His meeting with his family I leave the reader to imagine. The wilderness received him almost a corpse. It returned him to his home and the world as happy and healthy a man as ever bivouacked under its pines.

This, I am aware, is an extreme case, and, as such, may seem exaggerated; but it is not. I might instance many other cases which, if less startling, are equally corroborative of the general statement. There is one sitting near me, as I write, the color of whose cheek,

THE WILDERNESS

and the clear brightness of whose eye, cause my heart to go out in ceaseless gratitude to the woods, amid which she found that health and strength of which they are the proof and sign. For five summers have we visited the wilderness. From four to seven weeks, each year, have we breathed the breath of the mountains; bathed in the waters which sleep at their base; and made our couch at night of moss and balsam-boughs, beneath the whispering trees. I feel, therefore, that I am able to speak from experience touching this matter; and I believe that, all things being considered, no portion of our country surpasses, if indeed any equals, in health-giving qualities, the Adirondack Wilderness.

About This Story

When considering stories, we never want to select something out of obligation. Just because it's a *classic* doesn't mean it will work for our collection. Browsing the many small Adirondack town libraries, we noted that William H. H. Murray's book *Adventures in the Wilderness; or, Camp-Life in the Adirondacks* appeared to be a staple, but initially we were turned off by his "Loon-Shooting in a Thunderstorm" chapter as we thumbed through the pages. But when a book plays a major role in defining a region and inspires an entire country to get outdoors camping . . . maybe we'll give it another look. We chose this piece for the window it provides into what early visitors saw before the Adirondacks were a *thing* and because it demonstrates the healing capacity of its forests, another aspect of this region that attracted visitors far and wide after Murray wrote about it.

Murray was a Congregationalist minister who enjoyed hunting and fishing, and took his first camping vacation in the Adirondacks in 1864. According to an article in *Smithsonian* magazine entitled "The Minister Who Invented Camping in America," Murray's preoccupation with outdoor recreation was "generally discouraged" by Congregationalists "because they viewed these sports as undermining pastoral zeal." But Murray returned to the Adirondacks each year, often with groups of friends, to hike, canoe, fish, and camp. The article goes on to describe how ministers at the time were writing animated essays as a "narrative exercise" for delivering more engaging sermons, and Murray used this tool to capture his trips to the wilderness. His often humorous and cheerful essays were never intended to be published, but a good friend encouraged him to submit something to a Boston publisher, so Murray pitched a collection of his essays and the publisher went for it. The book, published in 1869, was an instant hit with readers, launching Murray into fame and wealth.

The book also launched a craze for the Adirondack wilderness, referred to by some as "Murray's Rush," making these quiet woods a booming tourist destination for "Murray's Fools," those who wanted to camp, hunt, and fish. Ironically, this Murray-made interest led to the creation of what we now refer to as the Adirondack Great Camps, lavish compounds and cabins that make for a very different wilderness adventure than the one Murray himself promoted.

Blue Line Medicine

ROBIN WALL KIMMERER

Heading north, following the tang of boggy rivers and the sweetness of pines on the air, I like to imagine that I could smell my way home, like a salmon navigating to its natal stream. Closer and closer, the aroma draws me like a magnet . . . sun on granite, black humus, balsam fir, and a faint whiff of yellow birch smoke. When I was a little kid, in the wayback of our old red station wagon with a canoe on top, I'd watch as the farm fields disappeared and houses became few, the forest thicker and so fragrant I'd roll down the window to breathe it in. My dad would call out from the front, "We're about to cross the Blue Line!" and I'd crane my neck to see it, looking for a painted trail through the woods or a line across the road. That boundary loomed large in my imagination. I'd come to know that everything was different on the inside of that line. I never saw it, but I always knew.

I remember the pride I felt when he explained that everything beyond that line, lakes and forests and trails heading off to someplace you wanted to go, all belonged to us. I felt unbelievably rich. With the mythos of public land, planted in my understanding, we were free to explore it all, unfettered. As we got older, I learned the origin of this legacy created through the Forever Wild amendment, which seemed to me the pinnacle of ethical behavior. We were grateful recipients of the foresight of thinkers before us, who gave priority to the life of the land. Every time we crossed the Blue Line, there was a sense of safety. Here was a place I could love with whole heart, without fear of losing it.

Sometimes, as we drove down a sandy woods road toward a camping place, my dad would glance off into the woods and ask us ever-gullible children, "Did you see it? We just passed Sunday Rock." Indeed, the woods were full of glacial erratics, covered in blankets of moss, but I never knew which one it was. He was a great one for stories and building on the lore of a granite boulder said to mark the boundary between civilization and the wilds. He promised us that after you passed that rock, every day was Sunday. Here there was no workday, no school day, no time but the present. How a calendar could be abolished, I did not understand. My family was not much for religion or Sunday school, but as an Anishinaabe child, I knew that this was where spirit and praise rang through the woods, every single day. I was not wrong.

What is now called the Adirondack Park has long been shared homelands for multiple Indigenous Nations of the region—the Haudenosaunee, the Abenaki, Algonquin, and Anishinaabe peoples, who had a strong presence here. The rich gifts of this landscape supported Native peoples with fish, game, berries, furs, and especially medicine plants. Today, healers from these Nations continue to find the traditional medicines thriving here. Every landscape has its own pharmacy, but the ancient forests of the Adirondacks are particularly rich in potent plants.

Moist, dense conifer forests make a medicine garden. The deep shade and acid soils they create impede many common herbs, but those who have adopted an evergreen, slow-growing lifestyle thrive. Growing close to the ground, they are vulnerable to herbivory and microbial attack, which they counter with the synthesis of potent defensive chemistry. The needled forest floor is embroidered with creeping plants like goldthread, partridgeberry, wintergreen, and others who produce physiologically active compounds, which are used by them and by us.

The oval leaves of wintergreen catch your eye with their waxy shine, emerging out of the duff. It has a pleasant taste when chewed and is a favorite trail nibble. It goes by another familiar name as well, teaberry, in honor of the pink minty berries that ripen in the fall. I usually gather a bit from a plentiful patch as it eases fevers that come with winter colds. But like many medicines, it is slow growing, so I take just a little.

The trees themselves are medicines, too many to name them all: white pines, red spruce, hemlock, fir, beech, maple, birches, aspen, all of which were known and learned from by Indigenous botanists. Colonist records show that when the French and British invaders arrived here, they were a sickly lot, many near death from scurvy. They describe how Native healers prepared tree teas for them, by which they were restored to health. Northern white cedar earned the French name *arborvitae*, "tree of life," for this salvation, which was provided by Indigenous scientists and the trees who carried the medicine. When I am across the Blue Line, I try to drink tree tea every day, a cup of fragrant white pine tea giving me a daily requirement of vitamin C and the knowing that our bodies, mine and the pine's, are united.

Yellow birch is a dominant tree in the Adirondacks, with its curly golden bark gleaming in the sun. Its aromatic inner bark, laced with methyl salicin, is a fine pain reliever and anti-inflammatory. Barks are full of medicine, from black cherry, which soothes a cough, to willows along the river edge, which are the original source of aspirin. Antimicrobials, fever breakers, diuretics, cough suppressants, wound healers, painkillers—all made by plants of the Adirondack forest. Even the fallen trees bear medicines, in the fungi emerging from their bodies as logs return to soil: turkey tail, varnish conk, chaga, and more.

In the summer I teach a field course in Adirondack ethnobotany, and one of the students' favorite projects is to create a first aid kit entirely from the plants at their feet. But before teaching them any of the plant properties, the first lessons are in responsibility—how to enact the Honorable Harvest, to practice self-restraint and care for the plants who care for them. The medicines do not belong to us; they are gifts of the land to be treated with respect.

The Adirondacks are a mosaic of forests threaded by lakes, rivers, and wetlands. The bogs for which they are famous are also revered as medicine places. Chief among them are the bog makers themselves, the peat mosses or sphagnum, whose bodies become antiseptic bandages when called upon. In fact, the English word muskeg comes from an Algonquin root, *maskek*, which is often translated as "swamp" but actually means "a medicine place." In my Anishinaabe language, the word for medicine is the closely related *Mshkiikek*. When you break that word apart, its deeper meaning is revealed. It literally means that plants are "the strength of the Earth," which is the source of healing.

The Adirondacks were an important healing place for Indigenous peoples and subsequently for settlers as well. In the late 1800s tuberculosis was rampant in crowded cities, and since there were not yet antibiotics, it was an incurable scourge. One of the recommended treatments to regain health from this debilitating lung disease was to breathe the cold, clean, conifer-scented air of the Adirondacks. Special "cure cottages" and state sanatoriums were established with wide sleeping porches so patients could take in the air. Under physicians' care, some recovered, and this health-giving element of the Adirondacks is part of its legacy. In fact, the iconic Adirondack chair owes its design to tuberculosis treatment. The shape of the chair was said to open the chest and promote deep breathing, taking in the medicine which is the essence of the Adirondacks. Anyone who has sat in a chair by the lake knows the nature of its medicine.

Those who pass Sunday Rock today are more likely to be suffering from illness induced by the contemporary threats of noise, stress, air pollution, and the hyperdistracted pace of life we have created. What if there was a medicine that could reduce heart rate, lower blood pressure, decrease stress hormones, quell inflammation, and elevate mood? There is such a well-documented treatment, which produces relaxation, sharpens mental acuity, and promotes a sense of well-being. We might call it Vitamin N, for Nature. The Adirondacks continue to be a healing place, where we can recover from those stresses and learn from the land another way to live, in kinship with the natural world, not in opposition.

In walking the aisles of the forest pharmacy, it's important to remember that not all the medicines are for us. The woods hold deer medicines, prescriptions for chipmunks, and cures for salamanders, too. Even the soil relies on plant medicines.

The "Strength of the Earth" not only heals us but heals itself. The Adirondack landscape holds the memory of an abusive time before the Forever Wild amendment, a period of rampant exploitation by unscrupulous loggers and miners who scarred the land. When protected from these threats by legislation, the land was able to begin healing itself with its own medicine of resilient ecological succession. Aspens and paper birch came to heal the fire scars, lichens found a way to live on mine tailings, and generation by generation the forest comes back, along with eagles and otters. The Adirondacks have been called the Second-Chance Wilderness. It was the healing capacity of natural regeneration and the medicine of human love for this place that gave the Adirondacks a second chance.

That Blue Line I looked for in the woods as a child marks an invisible political boundary. It is not a wall. The threats to land and our more-than-human relatives—air pollution, acid rain, invasive species, and climate catastrophe—can cross that fragile line. The Adirondack Park cannot thrive as an island, where inside that line ecological health is treasured, if outside that line it is not. If we value the medicine the land offers us so generously, we must become medicine for the land.

About This Story

If you travel to the charming historic town of Saranac Lake, you'll soon learn this was a place of healing for people infected with tuberculosis (TB). This tradition began with the arrival in 1873 of Dr. Edward Livingston Trudeau, who had become infected with TB at a time when there was no known cure. Without other options, Trudeau sought a peaceful place outside the city, as it was then believed a change in climate could potentially help in treating respiratory disease. Not only did his health improve, but Trudeau went on to become a pioneer in the research and treatment of TB. After Robert Louis Stevenson, author of *Treasure Island* and *The Strange Case of Dr. Jekyll and Mr. Hyde*, arrived here and regained his health, Saranac Lake became a sought-after destination for TB patients. Instead of hospitals, Trudeau and his physicians placed patients in "cure cottages," where they spent much of their days outside on "cure porches" taking in the Adirondack air while reclining on loungers, or "cure chairs"—a design that evolved to become the Adirondack chair. Later, Adirondack guide Fred Rice argued that TB patients would be best served by getting off their cure porches and out into the woods, and he guided one such patient, young city-bred Martha Reben, to camp on a remote lake where she regained her health as described in her 1952 book *The Healing Woods*.

But Trudeau wasn't the first person to discover the healing power of the Adirondacks. Indigenous tribes of this region have held a deep knowledge of its healing nature for centuries. After reading her 2013 *Braiding Sweetgrass*—a book of Indigenous wisdom, scientific knowledge, and the teachings of plants—and learning of her deep connection to the Adirondacks, we knew Robin Wall Kimmerer needed to be a part of this book. She is an enrolled member of the Citizen Potawatomi Nation and a student of the plant nations. As a writer and a scientist, Dr. Kimmerer is interested in restoration not only of ecological communities but also of our relationship to the land, making the story of the Adirondacks a perfect one for her to take on. We are still pinching ourselves that Robin offered to write a new piece for our book. She is quoted as saying, "I'm happiest in the Adirondack Mountains. That is the home of my heart," and the memories she shares of growing up visiting the Adirondacks highlight this deep connection. We are moved by the way she weaves together how nature's healing medicine grows in the Adirondacks, how the Adirondacks is a place to go to heal, and how the region has the "healing capacity of natural regeneration" for itself—a hopeful message that invites us to imagine how we may become medicine for the land *beyond* the Blue Line.

After Finding a Photo of Kensett's *Lake George, 1858* in the Paper

JUNE FRANKLAND BAKER

His painting of the lake named
for a king—time folds
back to this summer, our walk
among the Revolution cannon and redoubts,
then the village where tourists crowd
at doors of restaurants and shops,
and parasails towed by motorboats lift
over the water to shape
like ancient, perfect clouds.

Not far—Prospect Mountain.
Ascending, we look over
the Narrows, the Eagle's Eye, a busload
of prisoners working to cut back
that wild growth by our highway.

Mother tells us she and my father
in the thirties hiked all the way—
hours up a dirt trail
to the lookout tower. We drive
almost to the summit, park
in a huge, paved lot, but choose
not to ride the viewmobile, with its guide
and amplified music. Instead, we climb, finally
come out from the trees to worn-smooth rock
that holds now only the base of the tower,
the rest of the structure gone—
but our view still finding the lake
and range after range of preserved wilderness,
from this height still close
to Kensett, and to that time of the king
who never came to see it.

About This Story

Thomas Jefferson in 1791 declared in a letter to his daughter, "Lake George is without comparison, the most beautiful water I ever saw; formed by a contour of mountains into a basin . . . finely interspersed with islands, its water limpid as crystal, and the mountain sides covered with rich groves . . . down to the water edge, here and there precipices of rock to checker the scene and save it from monotony." Considered one of the cleanest and clearest freshwater lakes in the US, this massive 32-mile-long lake was among the most painted subjects in the nineteenth century, when Hudson River School artist John Frederick Kensett rendered a number of views of it, one of which is in the permanent collection of the Metropolitan Museum of Art. The lake played a crucial role in promoting early tourism to the Adirondacks and continued to inspire generations of artists, including the painter Georgia O'Keefe. Today it remains a driver of regional tourism while also serving as the primary drinking water source for residents.

Lake George was once home to the Haudenosaunee Confederacy, as well as the Abenaki and Mohican tribes. It is believed to have been named Andia-ta-roc-te, translating to "where the lake is closed in by mountains." When Europeans colonized this land, they gave the lake a series of different names. One was Lac du Saint Sacrement, "lake of the holy sacrament," suggested by a French Canadian missionary who was deemed the first European to view the lake. In 1755, William Johnson, a British Army officer and colonial superintendent of Indian affairs, named the lake for King George II—who never came to see the lake. Johnson also gave the order to construct Fort William Henry at the southern end of Lake George, named after King George's two royal grandsons, which today serves as a museum and site of war reenactments.

We appreciate how this poem by New York native June Frankland Baker illuminates the trivial and fleeting nature of place-names for some of our most beloved and significant landmarks, which in the case of Lake George ignores the thousands of years of reverence and stewardship by Indigenous people. While capturing the juxtaposition of forest wilderness and the busy hum of activity during tourist seasons in the Adirondacks, Baker's poem also highlights another important aspect of Adirondack history. More than fifty fire lookout towers installed on the highest peaks allowed the state to keep an eye out for forest fires for nearly a century, until they were decommissioned in the 1980s after new technologies and fire safety practices made them obsolete. Today, the remaining lookouts serve as radio towers for various state agencies, and many can be visited to take in Adirondack history *and* the great outdoors from way up high.

Woodswoman

ANNE LABASTILLE

Excerpts from *Woodswoman: Living Alone in the Adirondack Wilderness*

Season of Splendors

Autumn in the Adirondacks is a season of splendors. By early September, all the cacophony and motion of summer—outboard motors, seaplanes, water-skiers, tourist traffic, canoers, backpackers, sunbathers, swimmers—abruptly cease since most of the annual 9 million transients through our mountains try to cram their visits in between July 4 and Labor Day. Now the mountains and lakes return to their normal tranquility and wildlife again appears.

On a misty morning in September I can step down to the lake and find damp paw prints and a sprig of pondweed on my dock. One hundred feet away a trio of otters may be fishing. First I see the hump of a sleek back, then a curved tail, then two rounded ears and bright eyes—no, four—no, six. It looks like an animal 20 feet long with two heads. Where does "it" begin and end? Could it be the Loch Ness Monster come to the Adirondacks? The mist swirls in the dawn breeze and obscures the otters for a moment. Then it separates and I see the three animals leap fluidly onto the rocks off my cove. Each holds a bullhead in its mouth. In the hush, I hear the crunch of bones. Breakfast over, the otters glide back into the lake to play more monster games. . . .

· ✦ ·

On clear, frosty mornings, I'm awakened by the stentorian honking of Canada Geese flying low over my sleeping loft. They sound slightly hoarse, as if having just risen from their slumber on some cold and misty lake. All day, skein after skein wedge south, nudged by a north wind. As each chorusing group passes, I run down to the dock to count their numbers. By nighttime, still flying, the birds are unbelievably high. I listen from the dock again, bundled into a down jacket, gazing 5,000—8,000—10,000 feet up. Their honking has the haunting quality of distant French horns. My spirit soars up beside them. I imagine the mighty Adirondack Mountains dwindling into dark humps interlaced with quicksilvered streams and moon-spangled marshes.

How I wish to fly with the geese away from dreary November days, the "freeze-up," and cruel winter. Away from the loneliness, isolation, and anxiety bred by blizzards. Most every local person I've talked to grudgingly admits to an autumn apprehension. It is part and parcel of an Adirondacker's psychological makeup. The geese contaminate us with this strange depression on their southbound fight and cure us with their northbound. In between, we try to tolerate winter, each in his or her own way. . . .

My First Winter (Or, How to Be Lonely Without Even Trying)

After the November freeze-up covered Black Bear Lake with a sheet of pearly ice stretching uninterrupted from shore to shore, but still of uncertain thickness, I began trekking in and out of the woods. Until freeze-up was over, in about two to three weeks, I would stay off the lake and carry everything on my back through the woods. This included food, milk, mail, garbage, kerosene and supplies. The walk took half an hour without snow, up to an hour in it. Existing during this period was certainly harder and more time consuming than in summer and fall; however, it put me in excellent physical condition and allowed me to become better acquainted with the lakeshore around Black Bear Lake....

As soon as a test hole chopped in the ice showed 3-inch thickness, I felt it safe to start walking down the lake. First I cut a straight spruce pole about 8 feet long and hammered a nail through one end. If I fell through, I could lay the pole across the hole to either edge and haul myself out, or drive the nail end into the ice like a long claw to get purchase. The other end of the pole served as a sounding surface. As I walked, I kept tapping the pole ahead of my feet on the ice. Good ice makes a solid resonant thwang; rotten ice, a dull thud; thin ice, a high short tap.

The first week or two I was extremely cautious and leery about walking on ice. Some of my loneliest experiences on Black Bear Lake took place on those blue-gray, chill December evenings when daylight failed at 4:30 P.M. and snow showers sifted down from lowering clouds. I would walk home over gray glare ice with a heavy pack and my pole, wondering if I'd even have a chance for a second breath if I fell through now—or now—or now.

By Christmas, however, snow had blanketed the entire lake and ice had thickened to almost 2 feet. I felt cocky. I used my pole only to tap the frames of my bear paw snowshoes, which now became necessary for travel. Every trip was different and enjoyable. The lake was a wide white canvas upon which I created snowshoe patterns as freely as a finger painter. Sometimes I'd see dainty fox tracks curving around the islands, or a jumble of deer hoofprints around an open spring hole, or the slide of an otter on the bank, or the juxtaposition of hawk wings and hare paws near shore. Rhythmic waves of snow or streaks of glare ice might be sculptured by the wind. A blood-red, setting sun could throw immense blue shadows of pine trees across the pearly snow. Or a brilliant white noonday sun might turn the cover into a vast field of flashing diamonds.

That first winter I perversely spent Christmas Eve alone at the cabin, not having any family to join nor wishing to visit well-meaning friends or neighbors. Temperatures dropped to minus 26 degrees on my back porch. Hawk Hill later reported minus 42 degrees! The moon was full. I stepped out into this glorious night insulated with long johns, three pairs of wool socks, two pairs of mittens, a turtleneck shirt, Icelandic wool sweater, heavy lumberjack pants, and jacket with hood. Strapping bear paws to my boots, I took a short walk through the forest beyond the cabin. Small firs had become marshmallow mounds. The creek had vanished into a musical under-ice rivulet. Drifts were decorated with wedding cake frillery. In the intense cold, my harnesses creaked and my fingers tingled. Snowshoe hares slumbered in shadowy caves beneath snow-laden spruces. The black balsam clumps seemed to shelter hefalumps and other strange snow beasts. Birches and beeches threw parallel shadows on a blue-white snow. Every few minutes, a trunk retorted like a rifle shot in the frigid air due to the awful contractions of wood. Across the bare canopy of the forest, sparkling stars were strung upon brittle branches. It was a magical night—a night fitting to be Christmas Eve. . . .

Winter Today

Winter today is free and fun. It is ushered in by the first blanket of snow *and* the first whir of a snowmobile. Instead of burrowing into their homes like woodchucks to suffer from "cabin fever," natives are now able to get out and enjoy a social life. Many towns have experienced complete transformations. Snowmobiles bring fresh faces, conviviality, enthusiasm, and excitement to winter-weary hamlets. Devotees buy food, beverages, clothing, gas, and oil; they need lodging and repair service. Romance thrives on the heady sport. Within the space of a few years snowmobiles have made a direct impact on winter life in the Adirondacks, especially on my life. . . .

One night I joined a group of acquaintances from Lake Serene and whisked miles up the lake to a lean-to nestled under ancient white cedars. Inside, a barbecue glowed beneath venison steaks and hash brown potatoes. A bonfire, whose flames leaped higher than our heads, roared out on the ice. A picnic table was loaded with bottles of liquor, cases of beer, plates, utensils, hot coffee, and cups. Snowmobiles surrounded the lean-to and campfire like patient horses hobbled around a covered wagon rendezvous. Beyond us, the lake stretched tautly away to coal-black hills as cold as chalcedony. A twilight glow hung above the hills—an apricot band transfusing into lettuce-green into lavender and finally into the royal purple which precedes black night. A few stars were already twinkling. By their very scintillation, I could tell we were in for a sub-zero evening. Everyone ate and drank heartily. We clustered around the bonfire for good conversation and warmth, turning back to side to front to side. Our shadows around the bonfire loomed grotesquely like spacemen—bulky bodies encased in full suits, huge helmeted heads, lumpish boots, and gloves. After dark, some of the men took their machines out to run circles, races, and cut capers. The throaty whine of engines echoed and reechoed across the lake. Twin headlights and single tail lights weaved and danced like a snowmobile ballet. It was a wonderful, companionable evening which did not break up until midnight. We left dirty dishes, empty bottles, blackened fire, pots, and pans for daylight. Nothing would disturb them and they would offend no one remaining on the ice for the rest of that arctic night. Streaking back across Lake Serene, I felt dwarfed by the great fingers and streamers of pale green and rose which flickered on the northern horizon. The aurora borealis was in fine evidence that night and made a beautiful finale to our snowmobile picnic. . . .

The Breakup

The breakup is a prelude to spring. The breakup is a prelude to comfort. The breakup is a prelude to companionship. Through it, the lakes, ponds, and rivers are loosed from winter's rigid fetters—the ice.

I have never seen the breakup take place. Yet every year I watch for it, always expecting a great exodus of ice. Expecting a rumbling, crushing, tumbling, tilting, crashing, and scraping down the lake and its shoreline. But this rarely happens. Instead, it's a gentle, imperceptible dissolution with none of the stern precision of freeze-up.

Actually, the most exciting moment takes place a few days before breakup when a 55-gallon barrel placed on the lake ice melts through. Folks from all around Lake Serene have placed bets on this important event. Everyone compares the dates, hours, and minutes. My old guide pal, Rob, sage that he is, has guessed April

23 at 8:30 A.M. (a good solid average with the optimum time of day given). Jake, a pessimist, bets on May 1 at noon. Sally chooses April 30 at 6 P.M. I take an optimistic chance on April 15 at 10:15 A.M. The winner will receive twenty-five dollars from the local fish and game club.

Once the barrel has slipped through, the breakup is imminent. The eroded ice is rotten, spongy, and pocked with holes where melt water swirls through in miniature whirlpools to the great mass of dark lake below. My last few trips down Black Bear Lake are tentative and damp. Cracks are showing open water along the shoreline. The ice seems to warp and bend beneath my weight. The snowshoe webbing gets soggy, gelatinous, and heavy. I use an ice pole again, tapping carefully. Then, one day, intuition tells me to take to the woodland route until breakup is over. A few more days pass with treacherous "black ice" still spanning the lake. And then, miraculously, one morning there is blue water sparkling in the sun! It's April 25!

I shovel out my boat from under a foot of snow, haul up the outboard motor, screw in two new sparkplugs, and yank on the rope. Twenty-three pulls later, it coughs into life, disgruntled to be working again after a five-month vacation. The first trip down Black Bear Lake in April is like the last one up in November. The water is thick and turgid. The weather is raw and bleak. But now everything is reversed, especially my feelings. Instead of resignation to impending gloom, ice, isolation, snow, cold, short days, and hardship, there is anticipation of sunshine, green trees, visitors, movement, color, long days, and singing birds.

It must be the same for wild animals, I think. Beavers, otters, and muskrats are suddenly free to cruise on the lakes' surfaces rather than dive precariously from air hole to air hole under a heavy roof of ice. How *do* they find those lifesaving exits swimming through the murk of a cold Adirondack lake with 30 inches of ice and a foot of snow overhead? And what of the fish? Do they sense relief at the lightening, brightening, warming of water?

Loons, grebes, mergansers, geese, and ducks are migrating. Any day, familiar pairs will be dropping down to Black Bear Lake and Beaver Pond for the summer. I long for the shrill laugh of a loon at dawn. The Canada Geese have seen the open water and are heading northward, sure of a resting place come night. Their jubilant honking drifts down over the quickening streams, rivers, and marshlands.

All through the mountains, from steepest peak to lowest swamp, water is moving. Trillions of cubic feet of water have been freed. The immense watersheds of the Adirondacks are unfettered. The vast vegetative sponge is yielding up its moisture. Water is purging, flooding, surging toward the lowlands. Crystal drops are falling from ice-coated boulders way up on Algonquin and Marcy. Tiny trickles are gurgling out from under snow banks on south-facing slopes. From every height of land, water is pouring toward its appointed tributary or main river—be it the Independence, Grass, Cold, Opalescent, Cedar, Ausable, Oswegatchie, Boquet, Raquette, Moose, Beaver, Otter, Sacandaga, West Canada, St. Regis, Schroon, or Boreas—hence via the St. Lawrence or Hudson Rivers to the sea. . . .

Before summer, even before spring, we must put up with a period which is bleaker, if possible, than November weather. Perhaps it seems so because of my impatience to see flowers, hear birds, feel sun. One of my colleagues has described the Adirondacks in early April as "the Siberia of North America." And as Robert Louis Stevenson wrote in April 1888, while a resident at Saranac

Lake, "The grayness of the heavens is a circumstance eminently revolting to the soul."

Days go by without sun. Cold rains pelt on roofs. Snows are soggy and almost impossible for snowshoeing. Short, vicious snowstorms occur. Every morning I grit my teeth, fight off the frustration of being indoors so long, and try to endure another long day at my desk. Then, quixotically, one day of sun will transform Siberia into a Dr. Zhivago-land of glaring ice and flashing snow. I lie in my bikini atop a well-blanketed toboggan and get a prespring tan from the blaze of sun on white. Then, as suddenly, the weather turns bleak, raw, and rainy once again. My frustration level soars.

By early May, the rain has swollen rivers to flood stage. Taking advantage of this, a new adventure-sport begins. White-water canoers and kayakers throng to the Adirondacks, intent on running the most powerful and frenetic of our rivers—the Upper Hudson. . . .

Spring

I wake at dawn to an absolute hush. It is 5 A.M. No rain drums on the roof. No frost flowers etch the windows of my sleeping loft. A pure, pale, yellow incandescence shines in the east, backlighting the bud-bursting trees. Something is different. I lie awhile in my soft, warm cocoon, drifting between sleep and puzzlement as to what has changed.

Rolling onto my belly, I squeeze open the locks on the window and raise it for a sniff of the air. That's it! Spring! Spring has come!

I throw back the blankets, scurry down my log wall, shock the dog into a flurry of barks (at seeing me up so early), brush my tousled hair, fling off my flannel nightgown, throw on jacket and jeans, and open the cabin door with a smile—to spring.

She won't stay long. Spring, on her fleeting journey north, shortens her visits the closer she comes to the Arctic Circle. Here at 42 degrees latitude, she graces us with perhaps two weeks of her vibrant, fickle, fertile presence. Her timing is unpredictable. She stalls, calculatingly, for at least ten days after breakup, letting us suffer the Siberia-like dreariness of late April and early May. She refuses to linger as she does in Virginia, for example, coaxing cardinals into cheerful concertos and wooing magnolias into creamy blossoms.

Instead, spring arrives unexpectedly as today, announcing her presence only by a softness and warmth in the air which have been absent for almost six months.

The glow is stronger now and a pearly pink light tinges the hills around Black Bear Lake. Three days of spring sun and the trees will leaf right out, practically bypassing that lovely, innocent period of frothy, pastel, baby-tender foliage. Instead they will turn quickly into a serious, deep green, adult covering. There is very little time for immaturity in the North Country. Life is hard, rough, and sober.

A flute pipes from the gloom under the balsams. Here is one touch of purity. A White-throated Sparrow is throwing his heart into a sunrise love song for an as yet unfound mate. His liquid whistle, translated by unromantics as "Sam Pea-bo-dy," is one of the most beautiful sounds in the Adirondacks. Clarence Petty says it is the sound of the Adirondacks....

A warm trickle behind my ear interrupts my musing. Blood! What can it be? Did I cut my head in the woods? Then I remember. Black flies! It seems too early, or is it? Any time after the witch hobble blooms, the tiny flies can appear. Yet this one seems an especially eager eater.

Black flies are a scourge in swampy areas and a nuisance everywhere in the Adirondacks in spring. They can effectively depress outdoor activities for a few weeks between late May and June. The black fly attacks like a miniature vampire. Its bite is almost painless due to a numbing agent in the saliva. Only the females need blood, and they may travel up to 10 miles searching for a meal. Most natives acquire a natural immunity and feel only mild irritation, but some people react violently to the bites with swelling and itching, even shortness of breath. I usually experience a day or two of sluggishness, swollen neck glands, and lack of appetite at the start of the season, but that soon goes. Like most locals, I have my own defensive techniques against the tenacious insects. Miniskirts, T-shirts, hot-pants, and bikinis only offer the flies human flesh on a platter; so I dress to minimize exposure. I apply repellents liberally every four hours, make smudges while working around the cabin, stay indoors on hot, cloudy days, or do things outside at night when black flies are inactive.

The state of New York has spent millions in research and control work. For years the chief combat trick was to tie blocks of DDT in fast-flowing streams where black fly larvae cling to rocks and submerged logs. My friend, Rob, used to have a standing contract for six weeks every spring to put out blocks in the swift waters around Hawk Hill. Then the dangers of DDT were uncovered, thanks to scientists like Rachael Carson, and blocks were abandoned. Next low-flying planes sprayed our lakes and valleys with newer insecticides, some more toxic than DDT, and others almost useless. In the towns and hamlets, fogging trucks liberally sprayed all the streets, gardens, lawns, and golf courses (even children) with insecticides of varying degrees of toxicity.

Now the pendulum is swinging the opposite way. At Black Bear Lake, several summer camp owners have written to the Town Board protesting the spraying of their property and the lake. "We'll use birds to kill bugs," says one intelligent neighbor. I couldn't agree more.

Having taken this stand, to save birds, fish, aquatic insects, amphibians, and other animals which can be harmed by chemical sprays in our mountains, I pick off the dried blood and scratch, then I shrug my shoulders and say to myself, "So, let the little bastard bite."

The sun has set. A chill seeps out of the snow-damp ground and off the icy water. It pervades the evening with a gray mist. The peepers trill on louder and more incessantly. I stand up stiffly. After the day's euphoria, melancholia descends. From sun's warmth to mist's chill—all in one day—all in one lifetime. Spring will always be like this for me—fleeting—bittersweet.

About This Story

Anne LaBastille was an Adirondack guide, writer, and ecologist, who many describe as a "trailblazer," "badass woman of the woods," "feminist Thoreau," and "wilderness heroine." Her book *Woods-woman* takes the reader along on her journey from working at an Adirondack lodge on Big Moose Lake to building a cabin in the remote woods along Twitchell Lake. She once had to enlist the help of her community to move the cabin twelve feet when a lawyer, appearing out of the blue one day at her secluded dock, told her she was in violation of a zoning code that forbade building of structures less than fifty feet from the shore. The cabin is now on permanent display at the Adirondack Experience, a museum where we first learned of Anne and her life in the Adirondack woods. Her legacy lives on through her endowment of the Anne LaBastille Memorial Writers Residency hosted by the Adirondack Center for Writing. Here, writers can spend two weeks in the heart of the Adirondack forest at a spacious lakeside lodge. They hang out by the campfire, paddle, hike, go forest bathing, and write indoors and outdoors.

LaBastille's story stands out from a sea of writing by men who chose to live as hermits. Despite being barely five feet tall, she was a fearless woman who "out-Thoreaued Thoreau," as an article in the *Adirondack Explorer* put it, by building and living alone in a small rustic cabin without electricity or plumbing. There she wrote and wrote—articles for magazines like *Sierra* and *National Geographic*, two dozen scientific papers, and more than a dozen books. A fierce environmental activist and conservationist, LaBastille continued to stand for what she believed in on her passing, leaving her thirty-two acres along Twitchell Lake "forever wild"—ensuring it would be added to the 50,000 adjoining acres of state wilderness.

From her cabin, LaBastille proved an insightful observer of seasons that most visitors, or "flatlanders," don't get to (or care to) experience—late fall, winter, and the breakup of the ice in early spring. Her words convey not only the planning required and the difficulty of surviving Adirondack winters but also the beauty and magic of them. As self-identified *definitely not winter* people, we were grateful for the opportunity to ride a snowmobile over a frozen lake and tramp the forest just after a snowstorm with LaBastille through the pages of this book—and *almost* eager to experience it sometime for ourselves.

Maple Sugar Moon

JOSEPH BRUCHAC

Excerpt from *A Year of Moons: Stories from the Adirondack Foothills*

March in the Adirondack foothills. A feel in the air of things starting to stir. Days growing longer. The first light through the windows of my cabin on the southeast flank of Glass Factory Mountain waking me earlier each day.

I step outside, bare feet melting the gray frost on the deck. Spread my arms and breathe deep as I go through a series of tai chi moves. And though the land is still caught in the winter chill—10 degrees Fahrenheit this morning—it's as if the cold cannot cut as deep now. By noon it will be 40 degrees.

It's time to tap the maple trees.

Sogalikas. The Moon of Making Maple Syrup. Or, translated more literally from the Abenaki language, the Flowing Moon. For it is now Sigwaniwi, the melting away time: when the moisture of earth is drawn up by trees as they awaken to the lengthening of the days, snow melting from the warmth of the sun.

There are traditional tales of how making sweet syrup from the trees came to be. The simplest is that a squirrel chewed into the trunk of a maple. Someone, most likely from one of our northeastern Algonquin nations, had left a basket by the base of that tree and the flowing sap filled up that basket. Not a woven basket, of course. One that was made as we still make watertight baskets today by folding pliable bark—most likely birch—into a basket shape and pegging or sewing it together.

When that person tasted the water in her basket, she found that it was sweet. And then when that water was used for cooking, it was sweeter still.

The first white man to comment on making maple syrup was John Smith in the seventeenth century. He wrote in his journals about how the Powhatan women collected the sap from the trees by making a V-shaped gouge with an axe and putting a bark basket beneath it. After which they poured the sap into wooden troughs. Each morning they would take the ice off the top of the trough and throw it away. They assured him that the sugar did not freeze, and, indeed, Smith noted, the sap got sweeter each time they skimmed off the ice. After doing this several times they'd then boil the rest down to maple syrup.

It does take a lot of sap to make syrup. The rule of thumb is about forty to one—forty quarts of sap for one of syrup. One way it was done before metal evaporators was to put the syrup into a dugout canoe and then drop in red-hot rocks.

I remember the first time I tasted maple sap. I was with my grandparents and only five years old. We'd pulled up to the Ferrys' house. Three elderly cousins of my grandmother's. A brother and two sisters together, none of them ever married, all of them in their eighties. Ethel, Edna, and Pearly.

Edna was the one who came clomping up to the car. She was wearing knee boots, one of their late father's old red wool coats, a scarf wrapped around her head. Her cheeks were as red from the cold as that scarlet scarf. She had a gray metal bucket in her hands. She'd just unhooked it from the maple closest to the road.

76 ADIRONDACK STORIES

My window was rolled down and she leaned through it.

"Have a taste" she said, "it's sweet as a spring day."

I shrank back in my seat with my hands over my mouth. I was shy back then and a little afraid of anything new. Especially Edna decked out in those crimson colors.

Thus my first taste of maple sap straight from the tree was delayed. Though not that long. After we'd all gone inside the big old house, I waited for my chance. And while everyone was talking, I slipped out the back door to another tree where I'd spied a bucket hanging from one of those hooks I later learned to call a spile. I cautiously unhooked it. There was only an inch or so of sap in the bucket and it wasn't too heavy for me. I looked around to make sure I wasn't being watched, then lifted it up and drank. I mostly soaked the front of my shirt, but for that cold, wet, and sticky taste, it was worth it. It was as sweet—in a subtle way—as the breath of a spring day. I hung the bucket back up. No one noticed me slipping back in, even though the back door did slip out of my wet hands and slam.

All five of those old people were looking at the ceiling as I crept back into the room, my grandfather stifling a cough that sounded a little like a laugh. Nor was my soggy condition mentioned all the way home. Though my grandmother did remark—as soon as we got out of the old blue Plymouth—that I might want to change my clothes.

"Seeing as how, Sonny, you seem to have got some snow on you—in some inadvertent way."

Which remark set my grandfather to coughing again.

I imagine that by now the sap house behind the Onondaga Nation School (ONS) has been made ready for this year's flow. ONS is one of my favorite schools, right smack in the middle of the Onondaga Reservation that is itself the heart of the Iroquois Confederacy. (I'd say that Onondaga is right next to Syracuse, New

York—except the opposite is true. Onondaga, that place among the hills, was here centuries before any Greek name was grafted onto the land. Further, a good part of the city of Syracuse is on land still owned by the Onondaga Nation and leased to the city.)

I remember the first time I visited the ONS sap house where Native students, from kindergarten on up, take part in that old ceremony of gathering and boiling down that renews the bond between the people and the maple—the Leader, the Chief of the Trees, as it is called. It's at this time of year when the Haudenosaunee people give Thanksgiving ceremonially to the maple trees.

Dewasentah, Alice Papineau, clan mother of the Eel Clan escorted me back there more than three decades ago.

"This is medicine," she said, handing me a spoonful of new syrup, its color as golden as pure sunlight. "It's a gift from the maple tree. Drink this and you'll be in good health all the year. So we say Nya:weh, thanks to the maple tree."

And that was what I said before tasting that syrup.

"Nya:weh. Thank you for this gift."

Maple syrup is the first harvest of the year. To taste it, to drink it, is to feel your body flowing like those trees. The nutrients in that sap are truly beneficial. A spring tonic to cleanse you of all that has built up over the winter. Nowadays, we can actually buy maple water in grocery stores. But though I suppose it's good, it is not the same.

At our Ndakinna Education Center in Greenfield Center, New York, where we teach outdoor awareness and traditional survival skills, we host small groups of college students from several different schools. They spend a week with us, working around the property while we teach classes and provide them with the opportunity to learn about our northeastern Native traditions of survival and respect for the natural world.

One year when we had such a group, we were making maple syrup from trees on our nature preserve. We had a big pot over a gas burner cooking down the sap on the small open-air stage behind the center where we did presentations. We'd planned to turn the burner off that night, but the eager college kids said they'd take care of it for us.

"Okay," my son Jim said. "Just keep a close eye on it."

The next morning when we arrived at the center we found a group of distraught students waiting, heads down like puppies expecting to be disciplined.

"We're so sorry, we are so sorry, we are so sorry," they chanted—a bunch of penitent pilgrims.

They'd been playing video games and forgot all about the cooking sap. Not only had it boiled down to a black mass, it melted through the pan.

Jim took a look out the window.

"So," he said, indicating the small plume of smoke rising from our outdoor stage, "are you going to put out that fire in the floor now?"

That produced another chorus. This time it was "Oh, no! Oh, no! Oh, no!" as they rushed outside to pour water on the smoldering hole in the thick planks.

Jim and I watched their bucket brigade. Then we listened, not saying anything as they kept apologizing.

"It's okay," Jim said when there was a pause in the recrimination chorus. "It's just a pot and a few planks." He paused and then shrugged. "After all, you did not succeed in burning down the Ndakinna Education Center."

That attempt at humor produced another round of mea culpas.

When they paused for breath, Jim looked at them and nodded. "Okay," he said. "Would you feel better if we yelled at you?"

That finally got a smile out of them, and later that day they showed up with a brand-new cooking pot they had purchased for us—twice as good as the one they'd melted.

My favorite traditional story about maple syrup is the one told among our various Algonquin nations—from the Wabanaki of New England to the Anishinabe of the Great Lakes region.

Gluskonba, who made himself from the dust that sprinkled from the hands of the Great Mystery, was the first one to walk around in the shape of a human. He often helped the people and had the power to change things. It is said that he originally made the maple trees so that they would give the people pure maple syrup all year-round. All you had to do was break a twig and pure golden sweetness came dripping out.

But the time came when people stopped doing anything other than drinking maple syrup. They just lay on their backs, drinking maple syrup, grass growing up around them, no crops being grown, their villages falling apart.

When Gluskonba saw this, he was not pleased. He poured water into the tops of the maple trees and the people all sat up, spitting out that water, asking where their sweet drink had gone.

"You have become lazy." Gluskonba said. "This was too easy for you. From now on to get maple syrup you must gather sap, pour it into wooden canoes. You must gather dry wood to make fires and heat stones to drop into the sap and boil it down. It will take forty buckets of sap to get one bucket of syrup. And so that you will remember to appreciate this gift, it will only come once a year when the snow begins to leave."

And so it has been since then.

I've never done the kind of industrial maple sugaring that was perfected at Cornell University during the years I was a student there. It involves green plastic lines, strung from tree to tree, emptying into a collecting tank. Even, in some cases, using a pump to suck the sap out into those lines.

What I do is just the simple stuff. Drill the hole, tap in the spile (a hollow metal spike), hang the bucket or maybe a plastic jug with a lid on it. Then, the next day I collect the sap from that tree and a dozen others in another bucket that I then carry to the wide, shallow evaporating pan. There I cook the sap down outside over a woodfire—before finishing it off inside the house on the stove.

I never get more than a few quarts a season, but that's enough to share. Maple syrup I made myself was one of the first gifts I gave to my wife, Nicola, when we started dating. Maybe it made a difference. Better ask her.

And, since giving thanks to the maple is part of all our north-eastern Native traditions, I say these words today as I walk into the woods, carrying my hand drill, my buckets, and my spiles.

Wliwini for this time of year.
Wliwini for all the maple seasons past.
Wliwini for those that will come.
Wliwini to the Maple, chief of the trees.
Wliwini to Mother Earth.
Wliwini to Father Sun.
Wliwini to this sweet season.

Chickadee singing
a new song for this morning
everything waking

First pussy willows
white buds on dark branches
replacing the snow

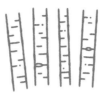

The Blanket Tree

JOSEPH BRUCHAC

Excerpt from *A Year of Moons:
Stories from the Adirondack Foothills*

It's early summer, near the end of the Strawberry Moon. I'm in the woods about to peel bark from the *maskwamoziak* as we call them in Abenaki—the blanket trees. Birch is their Iglizmoniwi (English) name.

Maskwamozi. Blanket tree. The one whose skin covered our lodges. I love the way the Abenaki words that first spoke themselves to the minds of my elders countless centuries ago, so often catch the sense and the spirit of the beings with whom we share this circle of existence. Know the true name and we may know the use, know what to be thankful for. Or, at the very least, better understand and respect.

There's a story we tell
of *maskwamozi.*

Once a little girl
was out with her parents
walking through the forest.

Her parents were quarreling
with each other
and did not notice
their daughter
had fallen behind.

When they reached their wigwam,
they turned around
to look for her
but she was gone.

It was growing dark
and then the snow
began to fall
as they looked for her.

All through the night
they searched for her,
calling her name,
fearing that she
had frozen
in the sudden cold.

But with the morning light
they found their daughter,
alive and warm,
asleep beneath
an old birch tree,
a roll of its bark
wrapped around her.

THE BLANKET TREE 83

As I stand carefully surveying the birch trees, I feel a sort of completeness here in the forest. It's a connection harder to make when I'm inside. Part of me longs to just stay here in the woods all day. Not just step briefly into the forest but instead remain outside the boundaries of clock time and the restrictions of responsibility to anything other than the ancient cycles of each season.

Interruption for a disclaimer in the interest of honesty. I am not surrendering to a fantasy of dwelling at one with all the happy little forest creatures. There are deer ticks and mosquitoes here. Also it is soon going to be horsefly season. Some part of nature is always willing and able to eat us.

I think back on my three years of volunteer teaching in the West African nation of Ghana. They were a reality check against my childhood longing, seduced by the admittedly racist novels of Edgar Rice Burroughs, to live as did Tarzan in the rain forest, swinging blithely, an overly muscled exemplar of the "master race," on conveniently hung vines from tree to tree. When I first set foot in a real rain forest, just off the road to Kumasi, I saw a hanging vine perfect for swinging on. I grabbed it—and the result was a cascade of fiercely biting red ants falling from that vine and on down my back and my neck. The long ululating yell I let out then was much like that of the legendary ape man.

In truth, only a part of me wants that forest fantasy. Another sizable portion is perfectly content ensconced in a comfortable chair with a pint of strawberry ice cream and reading. Or sitting as I am right now at my keyboard.

There is no such thing as an easy life.

But, having said that, there is also such a thing as trying to live that life in a good way. And for me that involves spending time as often as possible out in *ktsi kpiwi,* the big woods my grandfather first introduced me to when I was two years old. Which brings me back to birch trees.

I run my palms along the smooth body of the first tree that drew me to it, its pale, straight trunk is such a contrast among the brown maples and even darker pines. Its color is not the pure, untouched whiteness of new snow. It's a page marked by a black script written in a language that speaks of seasons and decades. An ancient language, it's one that speaks to those of us fortunate enough to have heard and remembered what elders shared.

On the trunk of the birch, upside-down Vs show where branches once grew. Those marks resemble outstretched wings, the sign of the Thunder Beings. Our Anishinabe cousins to the west see the thunders as immense birds with wings that spread from horizon to horizon, lightning flashing from their eyes. We Wabanaki know them as the Bedagiak, grandfathers who ride the dark clouds, hurling down arrows of lightning to cleanse the land of evil. They love the birch, and those marks are proof of that love.

I've been told (though white meteorologists view such Native folk traditions as bunk) that birch is the safest tree to shelter beneath during a thunderstorm. The Bedagiak seldom choose to strike it with their arrows. As if in proof of that, there's a lightning scar down the trunk of a big maple only twenty yards away from me, a tree shorter than this tall birch.

I look farther up the trunk of the birch. There's an ascending series of scratches, sets of four parallel lines incised into the tree, leaving little curlicues of bark as thin as tissue paper. Claw marks from the animal that climbed it. Not big enough or deep enough to be the sign of a young bear scrambling up. Most likely the porcupine I greeted near here a few days ago. If you know what to look for, you can read a lot in the woods.

I reach into my pocket to take out my tobacco pouch. Always make a physical expression of your gratitude. At least that is how I was taught. Tobacco is a sacred gift. It is only when misused that it becomes a harmful addiction. It was given to us to be shared with all Creation, to be offered as a sign of thanks, burned to carry our prayers up to Ktsi Nwaskw, the Great Mystery with its smoke.

We didn't always have tobacco.
Once all the tobacco
in the world was owned
by a terrible being known as Cols.

A giant creature
who flew through the air,
the sound of his wings
was louder than thunder.

Cols kept that tobacco
and shared it with no one.
He used its power selfishly.

Gluskonba,
the one who made
himself from words,
knew this was wrong.

He went to the island
where Cols lived.
All around that island
were the bleached bones

of people who'd come
to get tobacco.

Cols came flying
down at Gluskonba
the sound of his wings
like rattling bones.

But Gluskonba
grabbed hold of Cols.
Stroking him from head to toe,
he made Cols smaller
and smaller and smaller
until he was only
a grasshopper.

Then Gluskonba put just a little
of that tobacco into the tiny mouth
of Cols, so he always
would have some of that sacred gift.

But the rest of that tobacco
was given to the Alnobak,
the human beings.

To this day, Cols will sometimes
fly up and surprise you
with the rattling of his wings,
but he is no longer a danger.

THE BLANKET TREE

So it is today
that tobacco is in
the hands of the people—
who must always remember
to share it and use it for prayer.

I know from my own experience that it's always a good thing to give tobacco when you are taking something from the natural world. If nothing else, offering tobacco makes you pause, makes you mindful.

I remember a time two decades ago near Fairbanks, Alaska. I'd given a talk at the university there and had been invited to a reception at the home of my friend Jim Ruppert. In his backyard was a pile of birch logs cut for firewood. Jim gave me permission to peel some of that bark—as long as I didn't take too long since the guests would soon be arriving. I was in such a hurry to peel that bark that I didn't bother to make an offering or even express my thanks verbally. As I made the first cut, the knife slipped in my hand and sliced into my palm. I ended up offering not tobacco, but some of my blood to the Alaskan earth in exchange for that bark.

I take tobacco from my pouch. It's not commercially grown but *Nicotiana rustica*, the old Indian tobacco we call *wdamo wabanaki*. I raised it from seeds passed on to me by Tom Porter, a Mohawk elder whose Indian name Sakokwe-nionkwas means "One Who Wins." Tom is a man known to those fortunate enough to be in his presence as one of the most generous of teachers. And because it is important to always remember our teachers, it's with his gentle face in my mind that I carefully place the tobacco at the base of the birch.

Wliwini, nidoba maskwamozi
Thanks, friend blanket tree
Ktsi wliwini odzi kia
Great thanks to you

Then I make the first long cut from top to bottom. I press the knife into the trunk just deep enough to take off that top layer. When you girdle most trees, slicing through the outer layer of growth, you sever the phloem, that complex vascular tissue of sieve tubes and companion cells where nutrients are carried up from the roots. Strip the bark all the way around an ash, an elm, a basswood—and it will die.

But not the blanket tree. Birch can shed its outer layer without great harm to the tree. If you walk through the forests near many of our contemporary Native communities where there are birch trees, you'll see tree after tree whose bark has been respectfully harvested, wide rings of light brown wood showing where birches gave up their blankets.

All along the trail
I see the marks
of people who came
to these hills before me,
there in the remembering trees

People who work the woods can tell you that every tree gives off its own odor when you cut into it. Your hands and clothes and hair take on that smell. When you come home at night, you are bringing the breath of the forest with you. I remember how my grandfather smelled after a day of working in the pine woods. Moist sawdust stuck on his boots, his hands—which were already brown as earth—even darker from the sap of the trees, the woods scent all around him.

Pine is sharp and tangy. Beech is like peppermint. And the scent released from birch is a bit like that of beech, but not as strong. It's a clean, refreshing smell, as subtle an odor as the earth-making aroma of the cushioning layer of old leaves and pine needles beneath my bare feet.

I finish the vertical cut and follow it with two more around the tree. One at the top, one at the bottom, going from left to right. That's the direction in which to peel the bark. I know no other reason for this than that I was told to do it that way. Everywhere I've been where birch bark is peeled by Native people—Athabascans in Alaska, Anishinabes in Wisconsin, Penobscots in Maine—I've heard that's the right way to do it.

It makes as much sense as what I was told by a certain medicine person about the way to gather the bark from another plant I'm not going to name. Peel it upward and you can use it as an emetic. Peel it downward and it becomes a diuretic. Not exactly logical in the Western way of thinking. But who cares as long as it works?

The piece of bark I'm about to peel will be a shingle about three feet by three feet. No particular reason for that size other than we can manage it easily and there are no large knots or rough places in the bark within that expanse that would make peeling harder. It is plenty big enough to be a nice sized section of the covering we'll use to clothe the wigwam at our Ndakinna Education Center—the ninety-acre family forest preserve my mom put into a conservation easement twenty years ago where my sons and I teach.

I loosen the bark with the edge of my hatchet, begin to work my fingers up and down. And the bark starts to loosen. I go slow, applying steady, careful pressure as it makes little tearing noises, almost like Velcro letting go. Then, with a popping sound, the big piece of bark releases itself from the layer of growth beneath, leaping off the tree into my hands. A gift to be accepted and used with care, a good start for this day of peeling birch bark.

Peeling bark
my hands are touching
all those who touched
this tree before me

Two-legged and
four-legged ones
and those who fly

With a sharpened twig
I draw their shapes
on the brown inner bark

so doing, I know
their spirits will come
will speak to me
in my dreams

About These Stories

Raised in the Adirondack foothills, Joseph Bruchac is an award-winning poet, folklorist, martial artist, storyteller, and anthologist who strives to give voice to the voiceless and marginalized. A citizen of the Nulhegan Coosuk Band of the Abenaki Nation, he is the 2023–2025 poet laureate of Saratoga Springs, New York. His prolific contributions in the form of published writings, teaching, and creating opportunities for the marginalized reflects the wisdom shared with him by an Abenaki elder and dear friend to "give back at least as much as you are given." Bruchac and his sons, James and Jesse, operate the Ndakinna Education Center on their ninety-acre nature preserve, where they facilitate programs centered around Native language renewal, traditional Native skills, and environmental education.

His book *A Year of Moons: Stories from the Adirondack Foothills* takes the reader through each month of the year in essays that weave his own experiences with the teachings of Abenaki traditions and stories. We were drawn to Bruchac's essays on two distinctive natural symbols of the Adirondacks, maple syrup and birch trees, and their historic and cultural significance to the Abenaki and other Indigenous peoples who call the Adirondacks home. While many people think of Vermont when they think of maple syrup, the Adirondacks region has produced maple syrup commercially since the 1800s and ranks second in production in the US. In addition to maple trees, birch trees thrive in the cool, moist landscape of the Adirondacks. The durability and resiliency of the birch's waterproof bark have long made it a valuable resource for Indigenous people and Adirondackers in making canoes, containers, baskets, tools, and more.

The Lower Saranac

ALFRED B. STREET

Lightly flies my fleet bark across the glittering water,
Sweetly talk the ripples before the furrowing prow,
Mellow streams the sunset within the skirting forest,
Mellow melts the west wind in kisses on my brow.

Oh this life is glorious, this life within the wild-wood!
Far, oh, far away flee the troubles of our lot!
Wide expands the bosom, a boyish heart is dancing,
Dancing with the gladness o'erflowing every spot!

Dreamy like the past stands the distant blue Tahawhus;
Gleamy like the present, old Moosehead rears his crest;
Filmy like the future in front the bowery island;
Sparkling like our wishes the water's ripply breast.

Look, a wandering snowflake, the white gull in the distance!
Indian pink on pinions, the red-bird's darting glow!
Upward leaps the trout, and afar the loon is floating,
Dotting dark the sun-gleam, then flashing bright below.

Turn the buoyant bark through the elm's cathedral archway!
Nestles cool the cove filled with babble of the brook,
Sunny specks, and spice from the lily's pearly scallops;
So from glare of life hides some sweet domestic nook.

Onward then again, for the sunset now has kindled
Higher his grand camp-fire, and shines our tent before!
Crimson clouds are painting the purpled lake's enamel,
Golden gauzes gleam in the glades along the shore.

Onward, onward, thus do we press upon our journey,
Moved by restless longing, Heaven calling us away;—
Oh, may fading life be illumined like the sunset,
Beaming brighter, brighter, till darkness veils the day!

My Canoe

ALFRED B. STREET

You may boast of the haughty three-decker
That darkens the deep with her sail,
And the shocks of whose thunder majestical
Deaden the might of the gale!
How she crushes the billows beneath her,
The glory and pride of her crew!
But give me my light, little bubble,
My light, little, tight-built canoe!

Her curved frame is wrought of the fir-tree
And birch bark, the hue of the sun.
As over the carry we trudge along
Lizard-like, both seem as one.
Though buoyant as air, she is steady
When the tempest comes bellowing through;—
How she shoots, as the lake roars and whitens,
My faithful, tried, speedful canoe!

How she steals on the deer in his grazing!
And creeps to the trout in his sleep!
She vies with the pine-tree's soft melody;

MY CANOE

Wakening the lute of the deep.
When winter blears bleakly the forest,
And the water binds gray to its blue,
Safe and sound in her covert I leave her,
Till spring calls again my canoe.

About These Stories

On arriving in the Adirondacks and filling your lungs with its distinctly crisp air, you will find it hard *not* to feel the same jubilance captured in these poems by Alfred B. Street, who wrote prose and poetry celebrating the wild woodlands of his native New York. We first came across Street's poetry in the research library at the Adirondack Experience museum. Sixteen of his poems are collected in a book published in 1865 entitled *Forest Pictures in the Adirondacks*, bound in an aged brown leather cover adorned with ornate gilt lettering and illustrated with gorgeous engravings by John A. Hows. We selected these two water-bound poems to highlight the water-rich landscape of the region.

In the Adirondacks, water is life. Long before there were roads, there were waterways. The region boasts 30,000 miles of rivers and streams, and more than three thousand lakes and ponds, making watercraft an important part of the region's history and heritage. The earliest known Adirondacks boats were heavy dugout canoes built by Indigenous tribes who burned cavities inside felled logs and shaped their interiors with stone tools. Birchbark canoes (as well as canoes built with the bark of elm and spruce trees) later constructed by Indigenous peoples were more lightweight and spacious than previous vessels. These portable canoes transformed hunting, fishing, and trade, offering widespread access to this water-based terrain. They inspired the design of boats more than a hundred years later, including the Adirondack guideboat developed here in the early 1830s. Its signature ribs sawn from the "knees" (or roots) of spruce trees made this vessel strong yet lightweight enough for a single person to paddle it up rivers or carry it from one lake to the next—a portage, here called a carry.

One popular area for those who carry is the St. Regis Canoe Area, which spans 18,400 acres within the Adirondack Park and is the only designated canoe area in New York, an intricate network of lakes and ponds. The longest inland water passage in the US—running 740 miles from the Adirondacks to Fort Kent, Maine—was once a vital trade and supply highway for Indigenous peoples. In 2006 this route was designated the Northern Forest Canoe Trail (NFCT) thanks to the efforts of husband and wife Rob Center and Kay Henry. Building on prior research and planning by Native Trails, a group interested in studying ancient trade routes of Native Americans and early settlers, the two worked closely with Indigenous communities to ensure that the trail's Indigenous roots are identified on maps and trail kiosks and in trail literature, and that infrastructure and campgrounds did not impinge on sacred burial grounds. Additionally, since the trail runs through both public and private land, they made sure to gain grassroots support from local communities. The trail has now been explored by thousands of paddlers—including Laurie Apgar Chandler, the first woman to solo thru-paddle the 740 miles of the NFCT in 2015 at the age of fifty-three, a journey captured in her book *Upwards*.

Time by the Lake

WILLIAM CHAPMAN WHITE

Excerpt from *Just About Everything in the Adirondacks*

The little lake is blue under the summer sky, only marks on the old rocks at the edge show that four months ago the water was blanketed by heavy ice. In the wall of woods that edges the lake on all sides the yellows and the golds of spring are gone. Everything is deepest green. The wall is solid, without a break. Deer can stand just a foot back from the water's edge and never be seen. At any distance at all, aspens, spruce, maples, pines and birches are as one.

The woods and the lake are as they have been for centuries, ever since some ancient glacier gouged out a hole between two hills. A tree may fall by winter's storm but another one takes the empty space. Whatever man may have done here in the past with saw and ax does not show.

In early morning the lake lies quiet without a ripple. A noon breeze starts it shimmering and a full southwest wind in the afternoon sends little waves tumbling against the rocky shores. At twilight it is quiet again. Moonlight burnishes the water and deepens the shadows by the shore.

At one end yellow lilies bloom. Blue pickerelweed waves over them. On shore the pink of sheep's laurel comes almost to the water. Bluing huckleberries on trim bushes hang down over the rocks.

In shadowed places the new moss is fresh and green.

Warblers and redstarts flash by in the thick woods, their nesting done. Over the water, swallows dip and glide. A kingfisher flies low. A blue heron patrols one swampy spot watching for careless frogs. Now and then a loon comes from some hidden nest and cries a bitter, sarcastic cry.

Yellow perch and sunnies idle near the shore. A school of golden shiners moves by, popping at throngs of insects skating the surface. Bass that guarded their circular nests in shallow water are gone to the depths now, and newly hatched fry, a half-inch long, skitter in the shallows. Out on the lake at dusk a bass jumps with a noise that echoes all around. Without noise a mink or muskrat cuts a sharp furrow on the water, heading to the opposite shore on some urgent business. In evening a deer comes from the woods, in flight from the insects, stands fretful in a foot of water, and pulls at the lily pads.

Men come seldom to the lake, for it means a long walk through deep woods. When they do come they feel the remoteness and the distance from the troublesome front page. As a man stands by the lake he can sense more than that: everything is as it was last year, the year before that, as it was a century ago. That timelessness is in a museum but there it is inanimate objects that time cannot change. The lake and the woods are alive and filled with life but they, too, are beyond time.

Woods and lake do change but only with the seasons. Nothing in them or around them tells one year from another. One summer on the lake is like any other, like summers long gone and summers still to be. By the lake, apart for a few moments from a worrisome world, a man shares in that timelessness just by noting it. For those

TIME BY THE LAKE

few moments he can know it and be part of it, as he can never be in his own world where man-marked hours, days, weeks, and months count his years. He is a creature of clock, calendar and century as the lake and the woods are not.

As a man tramps the woods to the lake he knows he will find pines and lilies, pickerelweed, blue heron, and golden shiners as they were in the summer of 1352, 1852, as they will be in 2052 and beyond. He can stand on a rock by the shore and be in a past he could not have known, a future he will never see.

The lake and the woods give a frame in which the cares of a human summer, any summer, take on their own proper size. They let a man be part of time that was and time yet to come.

About This Story

William Chapman White was a journalist who formed a connection with the Adirondacks through his wife Ruth Morris, whose father, theatrical agent William Morris, owned a "cure camp" on Lake Colby. It was in the Adirondack Experience shop that we stumbled upon his book *Just About Everything in the Adirondacks*, full of vivid essays (originally published as newspaper columns) illustrating the depth and richness of this region. Reading this essay felt like a soothing respite by the lake after a long hike deep in the Adirondack wilderness. We felt the heat of the summer sun on our faces, heard the gentle waves lapping at the shore, and were transported to that Zen feeling many of us get from nature. We imagine it's these moments to which Adirondackers refer when they say there's so much to miss if you only summit the High Peaks.

White's reflections lead us to more deeply appreciate the "forever wild" clause of the New York state constitution protecting the Adirondack Park. Nature in the Adirondacks is as it was and will continue to be—this is *guaranteed* by the provision. Here you can allow your mind to imagine a future hundreds of years from now without worrying about shopping plazas or private summer residences around the lake. White reminds us not to take our protected public lands for granted, and how resilient nature is if we allow it just to *be*.

How the Birds Got Their Feathers

DAVID FADDEN

Long ago when the world was new and all parts of creation were learning their way on this earth, the Creator decided to wander the earth and see how things were going. It was a rather cool day when the Creator roamed the landscape, and he saw that everything seemed good and peaceful. The humans were preparing for the long winter ahead, making repairs to their longhouses, storing food, gathering firewood, and piecing together thicker clothing. The animals' fur was getting thicker, and some changed color to adapt and blend in with the coming carpet of snow. The brightly colored leaves had fallen to the ground, and the air had a crispness that was refreshing. The Creator was about to leave when he noticed a gathering of creatures who seemed in distress. As he neared this group and his view of them became clear, he recognized them as the bird beings. It was then he realized his mistake.

The Creator forgot something very important when he was busy creating everything on earth. He forgot to give the birds something to wear. The birds during these ancient days looked rather silly, contrary to their beautiful appearance today. They were pale and had bumps on their skin when any cool breeze came by. They couldn't fly very far without feathers and would hop around in an awkward manner when they had to move. They were not graceful at all. Other than their unsightly presence, the thing that really affected them the most was the difficulty they had to keep warm. During the cold nights, they would huddle together for warmth and shiver until the dawn. The Creator felt very sorry for them and decided to fix his oversight. So he went back to the Skyworld.

The Creator searched for something for the birds to wear up in the Skyworld. It was there he found a bag full of feathered coats, all colors and beautiful patterns. He slung the bag on his shoulder and brought it down to the earth, where he placed it on a mountaintop in the west. He wanted the birds to earn these coats in some manner. He then called for a meeting with all the bird life, and with his magical mind and ability he summoned them to meet. The snow was gently falling as the birds started to arrive for this important gathering. The birds huddled together, beaks clattering from the chilly air, and excitedly awaited the Creator's arrival.

The Creator found a hillside to address the anxious birds, and he began by acknowledging his omission. He told them, "I see that I forgot to give you something to help you as you live your lives on this earth. I see that you are cold and cannot fly in the skies. For this, I am sorry, but I have something that will make you warm and happy." He continued, "There is a bag full of beautifully colored coats on a mountaintop to the west. These are for you." The birds' eyes lit up, and everyone shuddered with excitement. They got restless and hurried to get closer to hear more, pushing and shoving each other to get a better vantage point.

He waited for them to settle down and told them more. "One of you will have to walk to and climb the mountain to gather the bag of coats. You will have to talk among yourselves to figure out who

HOW THE BIRDS GOT THEIR FEATHERS 103

will do this arduous task. Once someone is selected, this chosen bird will be the only one who can reach into the bag and pull out a coat to distribute." As the birds began to look at one another to figure out who will do this task, the Creator interrupted by telling them one more thing. He said, "If you find a coat and try it on, you can keep it forever. However, if you try a coat on and take it off, you can never wear that coat again." With that, the Creator disappeared.

The birds splintered off into smaller groups, and their voices filled the air. Who was going to get the bag of coats was the question at hand. Not one bird volunteered to walk to the mountain and retrieve the bag, as it was a long distance away and a treacherous climb up to the peak. Then, they would have to walk all the way back to hand out the coats as the cold weather was settling in. Hawk bragged that he could do it, no problem, because he was so strong and powerful. However, he declined and blamed his decision on a twisted sore ankle. Then the eagle, also strong and powerful, had to say no due to what he called a bad headache.

One by one, the birds found excuses as to why they couldn't make the trek. Their voices got louder and louder as their frustration grew. Before long, they were shouting at each other, and some began to shove others. In the midst of all this turmoil sat the turkey buzzard. Turkey Buzzard was a very kind and peaceful being who stayed out of the fray when things got heated. He covered his ears when voices were raised and closed his eyes when arguments arose. Out of his aversion to violence, he stood up and shouted above the escalating chaos, "Stop fighting, I'll go!" A hush fell and the birds looked at the tall, skinny buzzard with amazement. He really didn't want to go either but he wanted the fighting to stop.

Turkey Buzzard took a deep breath and began the long journey to find the mountain with the prized bag of coats. He walked for three days when he saw the snow-covered mountain that pierced the sky. With another long sigh, he continued on and eventually found himself at the base of the mountain. He climbed and climbed as the falling snow began to accumulate on his shoulders. He reached the summit, found the full bag, and rather than taking a peek at the contents, he started the long trek back to the waiting crowd.

Several days later and with several inches of snow on the ground, the shivering pack of birds saw Turkey Buzzard crest the hill and walk slowly toward them. Even though he was exhausted, Turkey Buzzard saw that the birds were desperate to find their coats and get warm. He slung the bag from his back, and it landed at his boney feet. He slowly untied the opening and without looking, he reached in and pulled out the most magnificent feathered coat. The crowd gasped with amazement and awe. It was a striking blue with a hint of white and black on the pointed hat. Blue was Turkey Buzzard's favorite color, so he decided to try it on. He felt the warmth of the soft coat cover his back, and as he was getting it all snug his eyes slowly drifted back into the bag, where he saw another garment that looked even better. He took off the blue coat and threw it to the ground, and now he could never put that coat on again. Blue Jay was nearby and quickly snagged up the coat and gave it a try. He loved it and was overcome with joy, letting out a loud, piercing yell. Now he could fly, and he flew all around with excitement. Today we all see the blue jay wearing that coat he tried on many years ago.

Turkey Buzzard reached back in and removed the most beautiful coat he ever saw, and the sounds of ohhhh and ahhhh hovered around the group. The most brilliant shade of red was seen by all, and Turkey Buzzard hurriedly donned the red coat only to have his vision drift into the bag once again, where he saw the most unique coat he had ever seen. He took off the red feathered coat and threw it to the ground. Cardinal was close and quickly grabbed the coat before anyone else could. He tried it on, and it fit perfectly. He happily took flight, and we can still see him today with the beautiful red coat that can be seen from a distance.

What Turkey Buzzard took out next was the softest and warmest one yet. It had interesting speckled spots of browns and grays, with a spattering of white feathers. It was very light and had an unusual head covering. He had to try it on. It was warm and cozy, but when he put the headpiece on something was not right. It was way too small and tight, which hindered his breathing. This was not going to work. He took it off, never to try it on again. Through the crowd of birds, the owl rushed, pushing others aside, to gather the discarded coat. He was so cold, he didn't care what it looked like and didn't even care if it fit. He simply wanted to warm up. He quickly donned the light and soft speckled coat and he, too, found the headpiece to be too small. Owl felt pressure on the front of his face, and with a "frump" the face turned inward, making his face very flat. Then it started to squeeze around his neck, making it hard to breathe, and his eyes got bigger and bigger as he found a way to breathe properly with his nice warm coat. That's why today the owl's face is very flat and his eyes are very large.

One by one, Turkey Buzzard reached into the bag and pulled out a coat. Each one was very nice, and he had to try on every one. Each time he admired the coat he was wearing, his eyes would drift into the bag to see what else was in there. One by one all the other birds were getting their coats and flying around the sky for everyone to see. The duck, geese, and loons each found their coats to be waterproof, and today you can find them swimming around the lakes and ponds. Some coats act as camouflage so they can hide in the brush. Other coats are very striking and grab everyone's attention.

106 ADIRONDACK STORIES

Turkey Buzzard reached way down to the bottom of the bag, only to find a hideous and foul-smelling brown coat. He chuckled and threw it to the ground. "I'll never wear that," he said. Again, he reached deep into the bag and felt around for his next option, only to come up empty-handed. He looked into the bag and saw nothing. He turned the bag inside out and shook it around, and again, nothing. He frantically looked at himself, only to realize he had taken off the last coat he tried on. There were no more birds waiting for their coats, and there were no coats left to try. His head turned to the last available coat, the brown one.

Reluctantly, he picked up the coat and noticed cobwebs all over the feathers. He cleaned it the best he could. He shook the coat and saw dust and moths flying everywhere. With a deep sigh, he tried on the coat. As he slowly put on the brown smelly feathers, he saw that there were threads hanging loose all over the garment. As he was putting on the pants, he heard a "riiiip" as the right leg of the pants fell right off. "Oh no," he cried, and felt the left pant leg fall off. He rolled his eyes and tried pulling on the headpiece, and heard the familiar "riiiip." The headpiece fell off just as the pant legs had. "Oh great," he groaned, and started to flap his wings to quickly get into the sky. As he flew around trying to freshen up the coat, he felt the top of his head getting hot. The sun was beating down on his head, and he had no covering to protect it. That's why today when we see a turkey buzzard, he has a sunburnt head and his boney white legs dangle behind him as he soars. He stays way high up in the sky going in circles so that no one can see how funny he looks.

That is how the birds got their feathers. . .

About This Story

While we as editors usually write this blurb, we wanted to instead reprint these memories that David sent along with his story:

I was very fortunate to have grown up living next door to my grandparents, Ray and Christine Fadden. They established the Six Nations Indian Museum (now the Six Nations Iroquois Cultural Center) in 1954 and welcomed visitors to the Adirondack Mountains from all around the globe. The mission was, and still is, to share the culture of the Haudenosaunee (Iroquois or Six Nations) with all who enter the modest four-room building. My grandfather, and later my dad, John Fadden, would use the numerous beaded pictographic belts on the walls of the second room to tell legends and other historical accounts. As a kid, I would sit for hours listening to my grandfather tell the tales of our ancestors. Before I knew it, I was the storyteller. It wasn't by choice, but rather I had a sense of obligation to keep the oral tradition moving forward for coming generations.

When I was twenty-two years old, I renovated a geodesic dome that my dad had constructed during the 1960s for an art studio. The dome fell into disrepair over the years, and I decided to make it habitable once again. I loved that place and made it very comfortable, complete with a coffeepot and a large window where I could sit and watch the critters munch on seeds and other delicious scraps I left for them. My woodstove kept things nice and warm during the colder months, and my grandfather would walk over and visit on an almost daily basis. I think he liked my coffee, and we talked about the events of the day. Most visits we would talk about the current state of the world and often during these talks, his words would turn to the natural world. In addition to being a world-class storyteller and historian, he was an environmentalist. After we had solved the world's problems, he would exit and go about his day. I looked forward to his visits every day.

One particular visit during a cold autumn day will stay with me forever. After I poured him a nice hot cup of java, he started telling me stories I had never heard before. I have a feeling he knew that due to his age, his days on the earth were nearing an unavoidable close. Knowing that I was beginning to retell the stories he told at the [Six Nations Iroquois Cultural Center], he wanted to teach me a few more to add to my repertoire. The first story he told me was a legend that was rather humorous and had a nice moral for the young listener.

The first story is the one that I share with you here.

Blinded by the Light

ELIZABETH FOLWELL

Excerpted from *Short Carries: Essays from Adirondack Life*

Light has remarkable, changeable qualities in the Adirondacks. In winter it can be pink, floating warmth over a chill landscape, or blue, tinting a blank canvas of snow to mirror an austere sky. In summer, light has depth and heft to it, a physical intensity that bears down like gravity or hauls a scene right into the viewer's eyes and brain.

The best summer days are those glowing ones, when all disheveled nature stands out in brilliant gilt-edged isolation, when the longest, widest vistas are as blowtorch sharp as the silver-burnished blueberries at your feet. The scales of a red pine tree aren't merely brown in this light, they're umber, rust and raw sienna in distinct oblong plaques, with deep greenish-black edges where they overlap. Or study the delirious color scheme of red-osier dogwood; out of the ground rises a clump of shiny, smooth, slender canes, with lime-green bark that segues to yellow-orange, red and finally deep maroon. Comprehend for a moment that the vermilion edge outlining a painted turtle's shell is close to the color of cardinal flower petals that ring the turtle's pond or the back of a scarlet tanager as he darts away from the same water's emerald border. Coincidence? Or reward for attending to detail? Think about the water of a favorite trout stream; the same gin-clear liquid that spills over your fingers transforms to weak tea, nut-brown ale and finally stout, complete with foamy head. Light connects, light separates.

There's more than color to Adirondack vision on one of these days, there's the orderly perspective of a chosen landscape, the way lumpy mountains pile up on each other, chaos at first sight, then foreground, midground, background, sky. The topography emerges so that we can build a mind map, plot that yes, this peak is before that one, or yes, that pond is nestled between those two hills. Imagine that view with the eyes of a dragonfly, each orb with 50,000 facets, each dragonfly brain capable of processing a hundred hues to every nuance we pride ourselves on seeing. Try those mountains from a peregrine's point of view, winging a hundred miles an hour above the highest trees—yet able to spot a chickadee darting past the forest margin. Vision must be true and trustworthy for that predator to succeed.

Sight is, of course, the prideful sense, the arrogant sense, and it's only fitting for humans to be so dependent on it. Seeing is believing. It's why we value eyewitness accounts. It's how we prove something to be so. But vision is a quick picture. Light travels too fast.

When it comes to the other senses, we're babes in the woods; our equipment is crude, our skills undeveloped. A barn owl can hear a mouse's footsteps and relies completely on sound to capture prey. Bats use sound not only to hunt but for navigation; sound distinguishes space from solid. These are specifics. Wild country is saturated with noise and song that humans are scarcely prepared to understand. The multitude of sounds in the woods contains as much meaning and complexity as a Mahler symphony, with bird

BLINDED BY THE LIGHT

notes filling in for oboe, flute, horn and percussion. I would love to stand in a clearing and hear the natural interplay with the same appreciation I have for music. I could learn, I suspect.

One thing that probably can't be learned, though, is to perceive scents like a dog. Smells exist in three dimensions for a beagle sniffing along a trail—up, down, over, under—but there's also the element of time. Scent is ephemeral on the wind, yet lingers on the ground for nose-driven beasts. This fragrance is fresh, from a bobcat marking his territory only hours before; this smell is older, a deer's bed of last night. These clues are important to a dog, historical information to be sifted out from the kinds of scent we notice: the must of rotting leaves, the hay-like perfume of balsam, the tang of pine.

"Viewshed" is one of those twentieth-century words that has a certain usefulness but no real poetry. It describes a pristine vista that should not be defaced. Someday we may come to value wild country as sound garden or scent sanctuary, worthy of attention and respect.

About This Story

We first met Elizabeth "Betsy" Folwell over breakfast at Chef Darrell's—a retro stainless-steel roadside diner in Blue Mountain Lake, New York. Betsy humbly failed to mention, until we arrived, that this was *her* diner—well, it was, until she sold it after its busy first year to the restaurant's chef, Darrell Spencer, who had trained at the Culinary Institute of America and cooked in New York, Puerto Rico, and elsewhere. While Chef Darrell was happily making conversation with and nonstop feeding my friend and travel companion—who attested that it was the best French toast she had ever tasted in more than forty years of semiprofessional breakfast eating—I was

ADIRONDACK STORIES

engrossed in conversation with Betsy, who brought an encyclopedic knowledge of the Adirondacks.

Betsy's deep love and sense of this place stem from her many decades of immersing herself in the Adirondacks by foot and boat; thirty years at *Adirondack Life* magazine as writer, editor, and creative director; and writing the first three editions of the comprehensive Adirondacks travel guide *The Adirondack Book*. This piece we've selected from her book *Short Carries*, a collection of essays from *Adirondack Life* magazine.

When we interviewed Nathalie Thill, executive director of the Adirondack Center for Writing, she insisted that writing without the *human* element is not only boring but also dishonest . . . it's not real. Nathalie described Betsy's work in *Short Carries* as a perfect example of that human element, writing distinctly as somebody who lives here year-round, not just seasonally.

As we were heading out of the diner, Betsy surprised me again by sharing that she's blind—a fact I had missed during the hour and a half I thought I was making eye contact with her while deep in conversation. Later, after reading this essay, I was curious to learn more about her disability and how it has reshaped her life in the Adirondacks—when had she lost the very sense she's writing about in this story? How has it changed her way of experiencing the park? Betsy was more than generous with her time and story, and we're grateful to share her reflections here.

I wrote 'Blinded by the Light' after I had lost sight in one eye due to optic nerve disease, which was quick and painless but untreatable. I did a short hike to zero in on particular things, like the scales of a pine tree, and that built out onto all the colors that are found on the simplest things in nature. I could have gone off on feathers, many of which are iridescent and change in different light. Crows can be silver, for instance, just depending on how sunlight strikes their bodies.

I have always been a person driven by vision. Just ten months after one eye quit, the other failed in just five days. The transformation was so rapid, with so many necessary changes to almost everything I do. And even now, when I see so poorly I try to frame my surroundings in a very visual way. It's how we communicate best, I think.

At first I thought this was a myth, that a blind person becomes more sensitive to sounds and smells. But for me it's true. Adirondack smells are so incredibly varied even for humans, whose noses are about one one-hundredth as acute as a dog's. In the late fall, the smell of the woods is dominated by popple, with leaves that have a funky odor, not welcoming like balsam fir. Pine on a summer day, when the sun's heat warms the needles, is so intense. Different waterways have their own scent footprint, depending on the vegetation nearby.

I listen a lot, too. I still paddle a solo canoe in the company of friends, and try to be confident. They direct me if I'm likely to hit a rock or veer off our course. When I do paddle alone, I orient to sounds on shore, like a highway or wind in the trees. And the sounds in woods and waters vary by season, with so many distinct birdsongs in spring, down to the lonely last wail of loons in fall as they leave our lakes for open water. So many creatures make noises that are initially hard to identify: a gray fox's bark sounds like a cough, a deer snorting the alarm sounds wheezy.

I hike now with poles since I can't see my feet nor the roots and rocks on a trail. I've pretty much given up on climbing even small mountains because the footing can be slippery, muddy, uneven. But old woods roads and many trails are still accessible to me on foot and skis.

I always loved going places by myself, whether hiking or paddling or cross-country skiing. I rarely venture out of civilization alone these days. I ride a tandem bike with my husband now since pedaling alone just seems dangerous. My outdoor activities are more social now, which is a different kind of experience, not quite so immersive but still important to the way I live here. Knowing that there are wild places within easy reach of home fuels my soul.

Loon Calls

ALAN STEINBERG

My heart stops
at the calling.
as if the sound
were older and deeper
than the nerves
that guard my blood.

I cease all conversation
all complaint,
like Job
at a voice from heaven.

At each call
I take heart, take wing,
for all the weight
of my soul,
for all the weight
of my learning.

If ever we could feel
sadness without suffering,
loneliness without pain,
this would be the song
we would sing.

About This Story

Mournful, haunting, otherworldly . . . the call of a loon makes all conversation cease around our campfire on a chilly autumn night. We're sitting on a small sliver of shore along Lake George, and we can't see much besides a frighteningly large spider—made larger by its shadow—busily building its web on a dim outdoor light, as we peer out in the direction of the lake, a black abyss. Spellbound, we sit in silence—unwilling to speak, for we might miss another—as if we're waiting to hear the call of a god, or ghost.

Common loons are iconic to the Adirondack region—walk into any store and you will find ornaments, tableware, books, art, decor, and really anything you can imagine with the likeness of this bird, its black neck banded with white stripes, its black body strewn with white squares and spots, like the stars in a night sky. Often we've found ourselves exclaiming to friends, "Have you ever heard a loon call?!" and failing to come up with the right words to describe not only its sound but also the *feeling* of its call. This poem by Alan Steinberg—which we first came across in *Blueline Magazine*, a literary journal that has published poetry and prose from and about the Adirondack region since 1979—gets pretty close.

Loons are often found on lakes or large ponds in the Adirondacks; you may spot them diving underwater to fish or using the water as a runway as they take flight. Their bodies are specialized for swimming, with dense bones allowing them to dive below the surface and large webbed feet propelling them toward their catch. As their legs are set far back on their bodies, they're not quite adept at walking on land. Despite their lineage being among the longest of all birds' on earth—with fossils dating back thirty-five million years—loons face imminent threats from pollution, fishing entanglement, development along waterways, and poisoning from mercury built up in the environment or consuming toxic fishing tackle. They are protected under the federal Migratory Bird Treaty Act of 1918 and are a Species of Special Concern in New York state. We hope the call of the loon can move humans to clean up our waterways and change our destructive behavior so that otherworldly song will continue to haunt our hearts.

Fish Stories

HENRY ABBOTT

Excerpt from *Birch Bark Books: Fish Stories*

Buttermilk Falls is one of the show places in our neck of the woods. The guide books make mention of it, and the tourist and "one week boarder" see it first. Also, when one tires of fishing, of mountain climbing, of tramping, and is in need of some new form of diversion, there is always "somethin' doin' at the falls." In the presence of their majestic beauty, and in the roar of their falling, tumbling, foaming waters, deer seem to lose their natural timidity and often, in mid-day, show themselves in the open to drink of the waters at the foot of the falls and to drink in the beauty of the picture. In the course of my wanderings in the forests, I have often observed in spots that are particularly wild or picturesque, or that have an extensive outlook, evidences that deer have stood there, perhaps stamping or pawing the ground for hours at a time, while they enjoyed the view. Such evidence points to the theory that wild deer not only have an eye for the beautiful in nature, but that they manifest good taste in their choice of a picture.

One day two black bears were seen feeding on the bank of the river just above the falls. A family of beavers have built a house about a hundred yards below the falls and have made several

FISH STORIES

unsuccessful attempts to dam the rapids, in which operations about an acre of alder bushes have been cut and dragged into position, only to be carried down stream by the swift waters. This is the only family of beavers I ever met who are not good engineers.

There is also the typical tale of the "*big trout*—a perfect monster of a fish," that lives in the deep pool under the falls. Scores of people have "seen him;" every guide and every fisherman who has visited this region has tried to catch the "wise old moss-back." Several times he has been hooked, but the stories of lost leaders and broken tackle that have been told would fill a volume, and he still lives. . . .

· ✦ ·

Sitting, one day, at the foot of the falls, I was studying the high-water marks on the adjacent rocks, indicating the immense volume of waters that pass over the falls and down the rapids during the freshets caused by melting snows, and spring rains, trying to imagine how it might look on such occasions, when a million logs, the cut of the lumbermen during the previous winter, were let loose and came crowding, climbing, jamming, tumbling over one another down through the ravine and over the brink with the mighty rushing waters.

The ground about where I sat was strewn with rocks, boulders and smaller stones, all worn by the ceaseless action of the waters, many of them smooth, others seamed with strata of quartz, granite or sandstone, some curiously marked and grotesque in shape.

As I sat thus, meditating, one of these curiously marked stones, about the size and shape of one of those steel trench hats worn by the "doughboys" in the late war, which had been lying close to the edge of the water and partly in it, suddenly jumped up and appeared to stand on four legs about six inches higher than it had been lying. The legs seemed to be stiff and the movement was like the rising of a disappearing cannon behind the walls of a fort. Instantly there appeared a fifth leg or brace at the back which pushed the rear edge of the trench hat upward and tilted it toward the water, when a telescopic gun shot out from under this curious fighting machine and plunged into the water. An instant later this telescopic gun lifted a small trout out of the water, bit it in half, and with two snaps swallowed it. The telescope then collapsed, the gun-carriage slowly settled back, the tail brace curled up under the rear, the head was drawn under the front of the shell, and the turtle's eyes closed to a narrow slit. Again he looked like the stones among which he lay, but his trap was set for another fish.

In a few minutes another young trout strayed too close to the shore and the operation was repeated. The maneuver, though awkward, was swift and every time a fish was landed.

The turtle is a good swimmer and he remains under water a long time. He doubtless also catches while swimming. This, however, was the first time I saw him fishing from the shore....

About three miles up stream, the beavers have built a dam across it, backing the water up through a swampy section about a quarter of a mile, flooding both banks of the river through the woods, thus creating a fair sized artificial pond.

Bige and I decided that this would be a good place to fish, but that it would be difficult, if not impossible, to reach the deep water of the channel without a boat. So it was arranged that Bige should take the basket containing food and cooking utensils up over the tote-road, leave it at the beaver dam, then go on to Wolf Pond where we had left one of our boats, and carry the boat back

FISH STORIES

121

through the woods to the dam where I should meet him about three hours later.

In order to make use of the time on my hands, I put on my wading pants and hob-nailed shoes and proceeded to wade up stream, making a cast occasionally where a likely spot appeared. It was a wonderful morning. The weather conditions were exactly right for such an expedition. I passed many spots that would have delighted the soul of an artist. He, probably, would have taken a week to cover the distance I expected to travel in three hours.

I had gone more than half way to the dam, had a few fish in my creel, and was approaching an elbow in the stream. A high point of land covered with bushes shut off my view of a deep pool just around the corner, in which I had many times caught trout. As I came near this bend in the river a most extraordinary thing occurred. I distinctly saw a fish flying through the air over the top of the clump of bushes on the point. A flying fish is not an unheard-of thing, indeed I have seen them several times, but not in the mountains, not in these woods, where there are fresh waters only. Flying fish of the kind I know about are met in the Sound and in bays near the ocean. Also, the fish I just then had seen flying above the bushes, did not have the extended wing-like fins of the orthodox flyer. This fish was a trout. I had seen enough of them to feel sure of that. True, I had seen trout jump out of the water, for a fly or to get up over a waterfall; but I never before saw a trout climb fifteen or twenty feet into the air, over the tops of bushes and young trees and land on the bank.

This was surely a matter that required explanation. An investigation was necessary, and without hesitation assumed the role of sleuth. Carefully stepping out of the water, I sat on a rock and took off my wading togs, then on stockinged feet and on hands and knees crept up the bank. Peering through the bushes, I saw that since my last visit a large birch tree had fallen across the pool and that the trunk of this tree was partly submerged. Sitting on this fallen tree over the center of the pool was a large black bear. Her back was toward me, and she was in a stooping posture, holding one fore paw down in the water. I was just in time to see a sudden movement of the submerged paw and to see another trout, about twelve inches long, go sailing through the air and fall behind some bushes just beyond where I was in hiding. Rustling and squealing sounds coming from the direction which the fish had gone, indicated that a pair of cubs were behind the bushes, and that they were scrapping over possession of the fish their mother had tossed up to them. It was, perhaps, ten minutes later I saw a third trout fly over the bushes toward the cubs. About this time the bear turned her head, sniffed the air in my direction, and with a low growl and a "Whoof," started briskly for shore, climbed the bank, collected the two cubs and made off into the woods, smashing brush and fallen limbs of trees, occasionally pausing to send back, in her own language, a remark indicating her disapproval of the party who had interrupted her fishing operations.

The mystery of the flying trout was now solved, but a new conundrum was presented to my enquiring mind; namely, how did the old lady catch them? With what did the bear bait her hooks?

I have told the story to many guides and woodsmen of my acquaintance, and from them have sought an answer to the question. Bige expressed the opinion that the bear dug worms, wedged them in between her toe-nails, and when the fish nibbled the worms the bear grabbed him. Frank referred to the well known pungent odor of the bear, especially of his feet, the tracks made by which a dog can smell hours, or even days after the bear has passed. He said that fish are attracted by the odor. Also that many years ago, he had caught fish by putting oil of rhodium on the bait, and that "fish could smell it clear across the pond." Frank admitted that this method of fishing was not sportsmanlike and that he had discontinued the practice. George said he had many times watched trout in a pool rub their sides against moss covered stones and often settle down upon the moss and rest there. He opined that they mistook the fur on the bear's paw for a particularly desirable variety of moss, and so were caught.

At this point in my investigations, I was reminded that a few years ago there was conducted, in the columns of several fishing and hunting magazines, a very serious discussion of the question, "Can fish be caught by tickling?" Many contributors took part in this discussion. There were advocates of both positive and negative side of the question. My old friend Hubbard, an expert fisherman, of wide experience, assured me that he, many years ago, had discarded the landing net; that when he hooked a lake trout, a bass or a "musky," and had played his fish until it was so exhausted that it could be reeled in and led up alongside the boat, it was his practice to "gently insert his hand in the water under the fish and tickle it on the the stomach, when the fish would settle down in his hand and go to sleep, then he would lift it into the boat."

This testimony took me back in memory to a time, many years ago, at a little red school house on the hill, in a New England country school district, where my young ideas took their first lessons in shooting. "Us fellers" then looked upon boys of twelve and thirteen years as the "big boys" of the school. We still believed in Santa Claus, and we knew that a bird could not be caught without first "putting salt on its tail." A brook crossed the road at the foot of the hill and ran down through farmer Barnum's pasture. In this brook, during the noon recess and after school had closed for the day, with trousers rolled up and with bare feet, we waded and fished. We caught them with our hands, and we kept them alive.

Each boy had his "spring hole," scooped out of the sand near the edge of the stream, in which he kept the fish caught. Of course, whenever it rained, and the water rose in the brook, these spring holes were washed away and the fish escaped. But when the waters subsided, they had to be caught again. Sometimes, we caught a chub as much as four inches long; and on rare occasions, when a "horned dace, a five incher" was secured, the boy who got him was a hero. It was the firm conviction of every boy in our gang, that, no matter how securely a fish was cornered between the two hands and behind and under a sod or stone, he could not safely be lifted out of the water without first "tickling him on the belly."

Reverting to the suggestion made by Bige. There would be no doubt as to the bear's ability to dig worms. She is an expert digger, carries her garden tools with her. She has been known to dig a hole under a stump or rock, six or eight feet deep, in which she sleeps all winter. I have, myself, seen a bear dig wild turnips and have seen rotten stumps and logs torn to bits by their claws; which was done in a hunt for grubs. I therefore felt certain that if the bear dug any worms she would not use them for fish bait, but would herself eat them.

With a judicial attitude of mind, considering all the evidence submitted, including my own early experience, I have arrived at the conclusion that the trout was first attracted by the odor of the bear's paw, then rubbed against the soft fur, when the bear wiggled her toes and tickled the fish on his belly, whereupon the trout settled down in the bear's paw, went to sleep and was tossed up on the shore to the waiting cubs.

About This Story

We first stumbled upon the *Birch Bark Books* series in the research library at the Adirondack Experience museum. The books had been set aside for us by the museum's director of archives and special collections, who upon learning about our quest knew we had to consider Henry Abbott. As we thumbed carefully through these pocket-size books, very aware that this was among the few remaining complete collections of the original nineteen volumes, the director shared how Abbott gave these books to his friends each year around Christmas to recount his adventures with his guide, Bige, primarily on foot and by guideboat. We were charmed by the birch-bark-adorned covers, the illustrations, and Abbott's humor—and particularly enthralled by the tales in *Fish Stories*, the sixth volume in the series, delivered to his friends in 1919.

In the preface to *Fish Stories*, Abbott shares: "An alleged humorist once proposed the query, 'Are all fishermen liars, or do only liars go fishing?'" While admitting that amateur fishermen may expand on the size of their catch, he suggests that an expert fisherman would see no need to lie about his fish or experiences, as "the truth always sounds better and in the case of a fish story, truth is often stranger than any fish fiction." We chose the fish stories that focus not on the escapades of humans but of the winged, finned, and four-footed creatures of the Adirondacks: "The fellows whose exploits are here set down, seldom mention their fishing experiences. They are not boastful, and never exaggerate. They do not speak our language. I have, therefore, undertaken to tell their fish stories for them." These include a cannibal "Grandad Pickerel" who swallowed his grandson whole, a pickerel who swallowed a watch that was found still running when the fish was caught, and a satiated otter fishing just for the thrill of it.

Wandering Home

BILL MCKIBBEN

Excerpt from *Wandering Home: A Long Walk Across America's Most Hopeful Landscape*

We set off on our descent, against a steady stream of hikers climbing up on the more usual route. Many were would-be 46ers, checking off another of the peaks on the list first compiled by Bob Marshall when he was a young man spending his summers in Saranac Lake. A staunch hiker, he and his friends tried to climb every high mountain in the park. Forty-six, he said, topped 4,000 feet, and these became the grail. (Better measurements showed he included four that didn't belong, and missed one that did—but myth proved more rugged than mere measurement, and his list still holds.) Many of the peaks on the list, Giant included, are glorious; others are grim marches to flat-topped mountains with no views that would never be climbed, were they not on the official itinerary. It's simple to make a little sport of the 46ers, especially since some people, upon finishing the list the first time, set in trying to climb them all in the winter, or to stand on every peak at midnight, or to visit each in the rain. But the quest serves two purposes: by providing that American necessity, a goal, it gives people a good excuse to get out into wild country; and it makes sure that the other thousand or so mountains are almost totally ignored simply because they're too low. If you know an Adirondack summit is 3,950 feet high, then you know you'll have it all to yourself.

In fact, as is often the case, describing something turns it into a magnet. Marshall was a born salesman—on top of one Adirondack peak he came up with the idea for The Wilderness Society, which in turn led the drive for the 1964 federal statute, relying all the time on the inherent appeal of the word. The 3 million acres of "forever wild" land in the Adirondacks are divided into two main designations, "wild forest" and "wilderness." The differences are very minor, having to do with grandfathered jeep trails and the like—but because wilderness sounds sexier, those areas almost invariably draw more hikers. Some conservationists worry that the High Peaks Wilderness in particular gets too much use, and there are periodic attempts to limit the number of hikers going up mountains like this one—require permits, some say, or build more parking lots and facilities elsewhere in the park to disperse use. But in fact one of the glories of the Adirondacks is that the high granite vacuums up most of the visitors, leaving the rest of the park to the creatures.

There were more than enough visitors wandering up Giant today, including at least one group communicating very loudly over walkie-talkies with other members of their party who were roughly, oh, forty feet away. I fear I must have been thinking of some cutting remark to make to John, because bad karma grabbed me by the ankle and sent me down hard on a steep rock shelf. Actually, the first part of the fall wasn't so bad—but a half-second later the full weight of my pack slammed into my back, sending me eight or ten feet farther down the slope and leaving me with blood streaming from both knees. No permanent damage, but I was sore and hot and grumpy as we plodded down the trail. I was,

I think, feeling my age, which is the only bitter thing about hiking peaks you've hiked many times before. The trail never seemed this long before, and it didn't help that granola-fed John was leaping lightly from rock to rock.

Thank heaven the path spills out on Route 73 right across from Chapel Pond, which is among the loveliest places in the park. In the nineteenth century, apparently, ranks of artists would stand by its shores almost every day, lined up behind their easels, trying to capture the rocky slides and steep, birchy draws above the pond itself. In our time this spot speaks most loudly to rock climbers—whatever the season, there's always a van or two alongside the road, and a few specks moving up the pitches. In winter, when a dozen waterfalls ice up, the crowds of climbers really gather. But today I wasn't paying much attention. All I wanted was to take off my pack and go for a nice long swim in the pond, kicking just fast enough that the blood trailing off my knees wouldn't attract too many leeches.

John had to be somewhere the next morning, so he actually allowed a friend to come pick him up in an automobile. I reminded him how such a contraption worked—the seat belt, the window crank—and then, feeling virtuous, gimped off to the east on the two-lane for half a mile till I came to the next trailhead. This one led south, and in less than a mile passed Round Pond, where I made camp for the night.

Round Pond is a lovely sheet of water set in a perfect forest bowl, and tonight it was graced by three loons, not to mention a small band of Christian college students. Nice as it is, however, it must be said that its name leaves a bit to be desired. I mean, come on, Round Pond. I've swam in at least four Round Ponds in the Adirondacks, and I bet there are fifty more. Not to mention dozens of Mud Ponds, and Loon Lakes in every direction. As a rule, Adirondack place names lack distinction. The problem, I think, is that there simply weren't enough people to create enough history; even the Indians mostly used the central Adirondacks as a hunting ground, preferring to site their villages in the warmer, more fertile land around Lake Champlain to the east, Lake Ontario to the West, the St. Lawrence to the north, and the Mohawk River to the south. They gave good names to some things—Tahawus, or Cloud Splitter, may have been their title for the Adirondacks' loftiest peak (or it may have been dreamed up in the nineteenth century by some romantic writer). But the first white guys who climbed it didn't bother with romance at all, naming it for the undistinguished governor William Marcy who had paid for their trip (and coined the phrase "spoils system").

At least Marcy was a *name*, though—for the most part, this is anonymous land, much of it named as if it had been inventoried by a warehouse clerk. There's First Lake, Second Lake, on up at least through Fourteenth Lake. There are so many Blue Mountains and Clear Ponds that the map index reads like a Beijing phone directory. As a result, I take it upon myself to occasionally rechristen particular spots with names I can remember. Tonight, tuneless hymns were drifting across from the campers on the far shore of Round Pond, an off-key bleating shamed by the pure clear laughter of the loons. "Shall We Gather at the River" is one of my favorites, but not in a Gregorian chant. From now on, I'll call it Bird-Beats-Baptist Pond. . . .

I camped that night on the northern edge of the Hoffman Notch Wilderness, along a stream known locally as "the Branch." It began to rain around midnight, and it was still coming down with some vigor the next morning, when Chris Shaw joined me for the day's trek.

The Hoffman Notch Wilderness is quintessential Adirondacks, much more typical than the High Peaks country I'd been traveling the last few days. It's pretty big—36,000 acres—and it's very lonely. Because the peaks stay under 4,000 feet, the trail register shows just fifty or sixty people a summer hiking the one trail that bisects the area. Except during hunting season, I imagine that the number who wander very far off that single trail might be counted in the single digits. It's empty, trackless country, unless you count the tracks of other creatures. Predictably, the main point of interest along the one trail carries the compelling name of Big Marsh; the biggest lake in the wilderness is known as Big Pond.

And Chris Shaw was the perfect person to hike it with, for there's probably no one who's traveled more widely and lived more deeply in these mountains. He came to the Adirondacks as a young man, and over the next decades worked as a camp caretaker, raft guide, ski-lift operator—always in a different town, a different corner. All the time he was writing stories and novels and articles, and eventually he ended up as editor of *Adirondack Life*, turning what had been a low-wattage tourist rag into an award-winning regional magazine. One of the ways he did that was to encourage actual reporting, which of course got him fired eventually, when he offended one (subsequently indicted) local power broker—but no matter, since he's gone on to write fine books since, and explore ever more deeply into these mountains.

So we walked up the Hoffman Notch Brook, admiring many small cataracts and moss-slicked boulders. When the trail leveled out at Big Marsh, the overgrowth was so thick across the trail that we might as well have been bushwhacking. The rain had ceased, but we hardly noticed, for every step brushed us against boughs freighted with water. Our rain pants and Gore-Tex jackets were soon soaked through—their main effect was merely to trap our sweat on this humid afternoon. I've been wetter in my life, but I've never been damper.

Never mind, though, because Chris talked as we walked. He's lived, as I said, across the park, from Stony Creek in the southeast to Rainbow Lake in the north, which are somewhat farther apart than Boston and Hartford. But, he insisted, there was something consistently Adirondack about them all. "The quality of the light is essentially the same. And the general feeling of place. It's continuous throughout the Blue Line—it's amazing how continuous it is. When you start to get up on the massif, the air changes and the light changes. Sometimes I wonder where it comes from—the rock, maybe, or the combination of the rock and the altitude and the vegetation. There's a very special time in the late summer, late August say, toward dusk. You're along shore on a lake or river, along that distinctive shoreline of mixed heath and rock. And all of the features click, fall in place for me. When that happens all at once it's like seeing your own name by accident in print, or catching sight of your handwriting on a piece of paper where you didn't expect to see it. There's a very powerful feeling of identity"....

By now we'd gotten past Big Marsh, and the trail had opened up some—it was an old logging road by the looks of it, from the time fifty or a hundred years before when the big hemlocks and pines had first been cut. People still work at some of the old occupations—cutting trees on the half of the park still in private hands is probably the most common job—and they've pioneered a few new occupations. (Shaw himself helped pioneer the park's white-water rafting industry.) But in general I think he's right. The days of the battle to carve a living from these woods are in some ways past. People here often live on money from away, either in the form of government payments or on their own money accumulated before they got here, or on the money that tourists and second-home buyers bring with them. Making a living off the land is no longer the common denominator of Adirondack life, and one result is that much of the land, or at least those parts of it below 4,000 feet, get less use with each passing year. The number of hunters drops annually, since many boys would rather do their shooting in computer games. And all of that is a sadness, precisely because, as Shaw says, there was an authenticity to those human lives that no longer can be matched.

In compensation, however, something else is slowly happening: the woods are growing in to a kind of deep and anonymous majesty. The nonhuman thrives. Here in the Hoffman Notch, logging once ruled. And when it did, other things suffered. The beaver had been extirpated from the Adirondack park by the beginning of the twentieth century, when state wildlife officials reintroduced a few pairs they'd trapped in Canada. Here, as in every other little watershed in the park, the beavers have by now completely reclaimed their territory—there's not a stream I know of that could support a lodge that doesn't have one. Behind their dams, new wetlands back up every year, their muck the single richest biome around. They buzz with dragonflies; frogs turn them earsplitting in the spring. And it's not just small animals: even the big ones, most of them, have returned. The moose have slowly wandered back in during the last fifteen or twenty years, and as we made our moist way through Hoffman Notch, we kept an eye peeled. It was a moosy spot, and if we didn't see one this day, we could have. Which in a tangible way makes this place richer, too.

WANDERING HOME

133

For me, the ecological story of the Adirondacks is more interesting precisely because it's *not* virgin wilderness. At one point or another, most of it has been cut over, sometimes pretty heavily. And yet, on purpose and by accident, this is one area where people have taken a step back. And nature has responded to that gesture. This is second-chance wilderness—not Eden, but something better. It's the Alaska, the Ngorongoro crater, the Galápagos not of creation but of *redemption*. No place on the planet has restored itself so thoroughly in the last century; while much of the rest of the Earth was turning from green to brown, it was going the other way. And so it produces an emotion at least as important as the sweet nostalgia that comes with remnant virgin wilderness. It signals to the rest of a deeply scarred world that, where we can figure out ways to back off a little, nature still retains some power of renewal. As we wandered farther south along the trail, the trees kept getting bigger, the understory more open, the beech trees more bear-clawed. Barbara McMartin, the obsessive chronicler of all things Adirondack, says in one of her guidebooks that this is among "the most stately mixed forests in the Adirondacks, making you wonder if it has ever been logged." A century hence, if we are lucky, people won't even wonder anymore. They'll just assume it's always been that way. They'll be wrong, of course, and in their error they'll miss much of the human history that Shaw remembers. But as errors go, it will be a sweet one nonetheless.

About This Story
Whenever we speak to locals, we ask what stories *not* to share about a place, to ensure that *Campfire Stories* does not perpetuate myths, stereotypes, or overhyped topics. In the Adirondacks, even people who have climbed all forty-six peaks and work on protecting land

ADIRONDACK STORIES

that provides access to these peaks told us not to glorify the High Peaks. So why did we include this passage? Because Bill McKibben pushes back against the idea of the High Peaks as grail, humorously pointing out that some are "grim marches to flat-topped mountains with no views that would never be climbed, were they not on the official itinerary." We get to follow him down to Hoffman Notch Wilderness, which he calls "quintessential Adirondacks," more typical than High Peaks country—demonstrating his, and the average Adirondacker's, point.

McKibben, who lives in Vermont, is an environmentalist and activist, and author of many books and articles that focus attention on climate change. His piece here helps us remember that before the Adirondack forest became state land, the woods reverberated with loggers felling trees and floating them down to the mills on rivers rushing with spring rain and snowmelt. "River drivers" had the very difficult and dangerous job of riding logs down the river and trying to prevent jams. Much of this harvest was utilized for building homes in a growing New York City, but some of it was exported to England and Ireland, where forests had been overharvested. The logging industry peaked in the 1820s, and often logging companies would abandon barren land they had cleared of timber. This allowed the state to repossess large tracts due to unpaid taxes—more than 600,000 acres of land in 1883, paving the way for the Adirondacks Park in 1892. To further protect this deforested landscape, the state government designated 2.7 million acres as "forever wild," which means that trees on lands within the Adirondack Forest Preserve cannot be cut for timber, and the land cannot be leased, sold, or exchanged. McKibben's closing thought about this second-chance wilderness restoring itself filled us with the same kind of optimism as Robin Wall Kimmerer's essay.

EXPLORE
THE ADIRONDACKS

✦

A guide for your next Adirondacks
adventure—on foot, by boat,
and up mountain peaks.

ATTRACTIONS

- (A) Cloudsplitter Gondola
- (B) John Brown Farm Site
- (C) The Wild Center
- (D) Fort Ticonderoga
- (E) Prospect Mountain Veterans Memorial Highway
- (F) Adirondack Experience
- (G) Great Camp Sagamore
- (H) Mount Arab Fire Tower
- (I) Six Nations Cultural Center

NATURAL LANDMARKS

- (1) Northern Forest Canoe Trail
- (2) High Falls Gorge
- (3) Ausable Chasm
- (4) High Peaks Wilderness
- (5) Mt. Marcy
- (6) Dix Mountain Wilderness
- (7) Hoffman Notch Wilderness
- (8) OK Slip Falls
- (9) Prospect Mountain
- (10) Comey Mountain
- (11) St. Regis Canoe Area

What to Do

Gaze upon mountain peaks from above and below.

While the Adirondacks are known for their High Peaks and many aspire to earn the title of 46er (someone who has climbed all forty-six), most locals agree  that visitors who only seek summits miss the very things that make this region special. They recommend also slowing down to enjoy what the mountains have to offer without climbing them. If you're interested in hiking the High Peaks, check out the relatively short trail to 2,267-foot **Coney Mountain**. Though it's deemed "easy" by High Peak standards, the trail involves a consistently steep ascent up to a panoramic 360-degree vista. For a challenge, hike to the highest of the peaks, **Mount Marcy**—also known by its native name Tahawus or "Cloudsplitter."

Another popular viewpoint is from **Prospect Mountain** near Lake George, which can be accessed by hiking trail or via a scenic drive. From the 2,030-foot summit, visitors can take in a sweeping view across Lake George and the Adirondack High Peaks, as well as the Green Mountains in Vermont and the White Mountains in New Hampshire. If summiting by foot, be prepared for a rocky 3-mile round-trip hike with steep inclines. The summit is also accessible by

WHAT TO DO

139

car via the **Veteran's Memorial Highway**, a winding 5.5-mile two-lane road with several vista points along the route up to the summit.

For a unique experience or if hiking isn't your thing, the **Cloudsplitter Gondola Ride** takes you on an enjoyable fifteen-minute glide up to the peak of Little Whiteface Mountain and can be enjoyed during the skiing off-season in summer and fall. From there, you can take in awe-inspiring views of Lake Placid, Lake Champlain, and the many Adirondack High Peaks. You can also enjoy the amenities at Whiteface—an apparel store should you need gear, a cafe for some grub, bathroom facilities for when nature calls, and miles of hiking trails should you decide you want to be among the trees.

Whatever you do, be aware that peak seasons and weekends draw crowds and fill trailhead parking lots early.

Climb a fire tower.

If climbing peaks doesn't get you high enough, climb up one of the many fire towers above tree line that were used as lookouts for spotting forest fires in the early 1900s. Now fire detection and observance are done in new ways, but many fire towers still stand and are a great place to get panoramic views of the Adirondack Mountains. The Adirondack Mountain Club has a Fire Tower Challenge, which invites people to visit at least twenty-three fire tower summits—eighteen of twenty-seven Adirondack Park summits and all five Catskill Park summits.

For a short and relatively quick trail to a fire tower, 1.9 miles out and back, visit **Mount Arab Trail** in the Tupper Lake region for a climb up the Mount Arab Fire Tower (elevation 2,546 feet). Here you can also visit the former fire observer's cabin, which has been turned into a museum highlighting the tower's history. For the more ambitious, hike to the **Lyon Mountain Fire Tower** (elevation 3,819 feet), the **Goodnow Mountain Fire Tower** (elevation 2,690 feet), the **Poke-O-Moonshine Mountain Fire Tower** (elevation 2,180 feet), the popular **Blue Mountain Fire Tower** (elevation 3,750 feet), or the less crowded **Owl's Head Fire Tower** (elevation 2,812 feet).

Get out on the water—by canoe or steamboat.

With more than three thousand lakes and ponds, and 30,000 miles of rivers and streams, the Adirondacks offer many ways of getting out onto the water. Consider starting by exploring the islands of **Lower Saranac Lake**, referred to by Indigenous tribes as the "Lake of the Clustered Stars," where you will find some of the most spectacular scenery in the Adirondacks. Explore at your leisure or paddle the route from State Bridge to Ampersand Bay and enjoy often-spotted wildlife like common loons, seagulls, great blue herons, and eagles.

The Adirondacks Park is home to the **St. Regis Canoe Area**, New York's only designated canoe area, which spans 18,400 acres and is the largest wilderness canoe area in the northeastern United States. In this intricate network of lakes and ponds, most of which are accessible only by portaging or carrying, primitive tent sites are available for those who set out on overnight trips.

The park is also the start of the **Northern Forest Canoe Trail (NFCT)**, a 740-mile paddle trail that runs all the way up to Kent, Maine—the longest inland water passage in the US. While the trail can be enjoyed if you have just an evening or a weekend, some set out to paddle the entire length of it, which takes one to two months—each section of it taking three to five days. The

trail winds paddlers through twenty-three rivers and streams, fifty-nine lakes and ponds, secluded islands, and rough rapids. It rewards thru-paddlers with adventure and solitude among serene landscapes and unforgettable encounters with wildlife—like spotting moose vegging out along riverbanks or falling asleep to the sound of a loon call.

If paddling is not your thing, there are plenty of other ways to enjoy the abundant waterways here. Operating for more than two hundred years, the **Lake George Steamboat Company** has a fleet of historic ships, including the Minne-Ha-Ha, one of the last steam paddle wheelers in America. From late spring through early fall, the fleet offers one-hour to several-hour cruises and an array of options based on your interests, whether a narrated cruise, dining, live music, or even fireworks.

Listen to a loon call.

Whether or not you're a birder, being in the presence of a loon at nightfall is an otherworldly, hauntingly beautiful experience. Common loons are iconic in the Adirondack region and recognizable by their striped neck band and backs speckled like the night sky. With bodies not designed for walking on land, loons need long runways on water to fly, so your best bet to spot or hear a loon is near one of the many lakes or ponds in the Adirondack region. Notice the different kinds of calls they have—you may hear a hoot, a wail, a tremolo (a "laughing" call), or a yodel, each with its own distinct meaning. If you're hooked, you can visit the **Adirondack Center for Loon Conservation** in Saranac Lake to learn more and support this unique bird.

Go fish!

The Adirondack Mountains have long been a storied destination for fishing—including fly fishing for trout in the Ausable River and fishing for bass, walleye, landlocked salmon, trout, and pike in the region's lakes. The abundant waterways offer a range of opportunities for people of all experience levels to fish for the many species that inhabit the lakes, ponds, rivers, and streams of this region. For some, fishing in the remote backcountry wilderness areas of the Adirondacks is a spiritual journey. Here, fishermen hope to catch brook trout, a striking species of native trout that is perhaps as iconic as the loon in the region.

If you'd like to dip your toes, or rod, into the world of trout fishing, you'll want to visit the **St. Regis Canoe Area, Pharaoh Lake Wilderness,** or **West Canada Lake Wilderness**. Or try out ice fishing in the winter in **Lake George**, where you can catch northern pike, walleye, tiger muskie, lake trout, brown trout, rainbow trout, landlocked salmon, and a variety of panfish. If you're lucky, you might just catch a 20-pound fish! Be sure to familiarize yourself with the rules and regulations for specific species, seasons, and bodies of water before you go.

Chase some waterfalls.

Not only is the region dotted with lakes and ponds, it's also flowing with many falls, tall and small, offering stunning views and ways to cool off in the mist. For an easy and accessible stroll, check out **High Falls Gorge** just north of Lake Placid. At this family-friendly destination, children, grandparents, and people of varying abilities can enjoy waterfalls and nature trails, and then browse the gift shop, nosh in the cafe, and use bathroom facilities. For the price of admission, families can traverse several sets of stairs and bridges overlooking the West Branch of the Ausable River and four of its waterfalls.

For a greater challenge, hike out to **OK Slip Falls**, among the highest waterfalls in the region at 250 feet. This ambitious 6.4-mile out-and-back hike will be worth your time, as it's not only an impressive waterfall but also an area frequented by moose in the wetlands. Keep your eyes out for moose tracks in the understory, and while looking down notice the mosses, fungi, and, if the season aligns, gorgeous wildflowers that blanket this trail.

An even more strenuous hike will take you to **Rainbow Falls** in the High Peaks Wilderness, located on the private land of the **Adirondack Mountain Reserve (AMR)** and requiring a reservation to visit. Go there in the winter for the stunning frozen falls and throughout the rest of the year for its namesake rainbows when the sun hits the mist just right. The trail to this popular waterfall is anywhere from 9 to 12 miles round-trip, depending on the trail you take, and can be extremely muddy and slippery, so it's important to dress and pack accordingly.

Take in local history, culture, and heritage.

You can easily spend an entire day (or two!) at the **Adirondack Experience**, a museum in Blue Mountain Lake that surprised us by turning out to be one of our favorite stops in the Adirondacks. Interactive permanent and rotating exhibitions span multiple buildings on a campus dedicated to preserving and interpreting the diverse stories of Adirondack history, culture, and people, as well as sparking thoughtful dialogue about the Adirondacks of the future. Grab some

144   EXPLORE THE ADIRONDACKS

food and coffee to enjoy on the patio overlooking Blue Mountain Lake and take in the stunning vista.

To visit a piece of little-known and forgotten history, be sure to stop at the **John Brown Farm State Historic Site** in North Elba when you're traveling to Lake Placid. Here you can see the home and grave of this well-known abolitionist. The farm was once part of the historic Black settlement that Brown referred to as Timbuctoo.

Akwesasne Mohawk artist, author, and storyteller Dave Fadden (featured in this book) runs the **Six Nations Iroquois Cultural Center** in Onchiota, started by his grandfather Ray. Here you can take in the stories, artifacts, and culture of the Six Nations of the Iroquois Confederacy, or Haudenosaunee. It's a place to educate yourself on the land ethic of the Haudenosaunee, environmental sensitivities, and the contemporary realities and potential futures of Native Nations.

Save time to play, explore, and learn at **The Wild Center** in Tupper Lake, a science-based museum with a mission to ignite an enduring passion for the Adirondacks where people and nature can thrive together. Here you can traverse the treetops on the Wild Walk, watch your kids play in nature at the Pines Wild Play Area, participate in a guided canoe trip, listen to a symphony of Forest Music, go for a hike across the 115-acre campus, or enjoy indoor activities like animal encounters, educational films, and exhibits on climate science, local species, and our planet.

Enjoy local literature or write your own.

The Adirondacks is a place that inspires literature, so it makes perfect sense the region boasts many shops featuring extensive Adirondack book and guide selections, such as the marvelous **Bookstore Plus**

WHAT TO DO

in Lake Placid and the **Adirondack Experience** gift shop, which also features an extensive regional book selection. While you're in town, chances are you'll be able to attend a book talk, workshop, or literary festival hosted by the **Adirondack Center for Writing**, a bustling nonprofit in Saranac Lake whose mission is to inspire the love of writing, reading, and storytelling. Or you can simply relax in their welcoming brick and mortar "storefront" to read books by local authors or try your own hand at writing about those lakes and mountain peaks.

Satisfy your sweet tooth with maple syrup.

Maple sugaring is a quintessential Adirondack tradition that happens every year after the big winter thaw in the maple tree groves, also known as sugar bushes. While this "liquid gold" can be enjoyed year-round, during the two weekends of the **Maple Weekend** festival every March sugarhouses across the Adirondacks are open for tastings, tours, and educational programs. No matter the time of year, make sure to stop by a sugarhouse or sugar shack along your route—there are a lot of them throughout the Adirondacks. We stopped by **South Meadow Farm** in Lake Placid as we made our way home, making sure to stock up on a gallon of syrup, maple candies (even maple cotton candy for our kiddos), and other maple-infused goodies.

Stay at a Great Camp.

Explore the life of rustic luxury at an Adirondack Great Camp, where you can take in history and get a glimpse into how the Vanderbilts, Rockefellers, and Carnegies experienced these mountains. Take time to admire Great Camp architecture and interior design, meant to reflect the natural textures native to this region—typically logs, stone, birch bark, and decorative branches. Many remaining Great Camps offer historic walking tours, guided hikes and paddles, horse-drawn wagon rides, educational programs, camping, summer camps, and overnight lodging. Try **White Pine Camp** overlooking Lake Osgood, **Eagle Island Camp** on Saranac Lake, **Camp Santanoni** in Newcomb, **Great Camp Sagamore** on Raquette Lake, **Lake Kora** near Raquette Lake, **The Hedges** on Blue Mountain Lake, and **The Waldheim** on Big Moose Lake.

Explore the Champlain Valley.

North of the popular destinations of Lake George and Lake Placid, along the eastern edge of the park and bordered on its opposite side by the Green Mountains of Vermont, is the Adirondacks' largest lake, **Lake Champlain**, sometimes referred to as "the sixth Great Lake." This region offers a trove of stunning scenery, small towns, and recreational opportunities. A premiere fishing destination and one of the top bass fisheries, Lake Champlain has some of the best catches in the region in any season—including ice fishing in the winter. If your arms are tired from paddling the Adirondacks' endless waterways, let the wind of this enormous lake carry you—hop on a sailboat with **Sail Adirondacks**, based in Port Henry, and admire the **Lake Champlain Bridge**, which you can also bike or walk across. Float through the **Ausable Chasm**, which some call the "Grand Canyon of the Adirondacks," one of the first organized tourist attractions in North America.

By land, drive the **Lake Champlain Byway** along the eastern edge of the lake in Vermont or hop on a bike to take in views of Lake

WHAT TO DO

Champlain and the High Peaks from the **Champlain Bikeway** and the **Champlain Valley Trail** section of the **Empire State Trail**, which run along Lake Champlain's western edge in New York. Keep in mind that the latter is on-road and traverses hills, so riders should feel confident in their physical abilities and comfort sharing the road with vehicles. Learn about history at **Fort Ticonderoga** and **Crown Point**, both military strongholds that played an important role during the French and Indian War and the American Revolutionary War. For hidden history, learn about the important role the Adirondacks played in the Underground Railroad at the **North Star Underground Railroad Museum**.

How to Visit Well

Leave no trace.

Seven and a half million people visit the Adirondacks each year, soaking in the sun in the summer and frolicking in the snow in the winter. Because these mountains and lakes see a high volume of use with little time to rest, it's all the more important for visitors to treat this landscape with care and recreate responsibly. Leave the natural environment as you found it, pack out trash and dispose properly, park only in designated areas, and avoid campfires above 4,000 feet or in areas where fires are not permitted. Water is vital to this region, and you can help keep it clean by not washing yourself, clothing, or dishes with soap within 150 feet of water. Trails can see a high volume of visitors, so be sure to always stay on the trail and walk single file, particularly when trails are crowded.

Familiarize yourself with where you can and can't camp on Adirondack land. Backcountry camping is allowed on Forest Preserve lands in the Adirondacks and other state forest lands outside the preserve, but prohibited within 150 feet of any road, trail, spring, stream, pond, or other body of water except at areas designated by a "Camp Here" disk. Camping is also prohibited in designated Unique Areas, Wildlife Management Areas, and a few other categories of state land. Visit the New York State Department of Environmental Conservation (NYS DEC) and the Adirondack Park Agency (APA) websites for further information.

Support nonprofits and land trusts.

Local land trusts and nonprofits play a significant role in keeping the Adirondacks "forever wild"—conserving critical lands that protect the public water supply, protecting scenic views and wildlife habitat, and maintaining hiking and biking trails. This includes organizations like the **Adirondack Land Trust**, which conserves and protects ecologically significant lands, working farms, forests, and wildlife habitats within the park, and the **Adirondack Mountain Club**, which promotes responsible outdoor recreation, conservation, and education through guided trips, trail maintenance, and advocacy efforts. Organizations like the **Adirondack Loon Conservancy** protect the wildlife unique to this region, conserving species and habitats through research, monitoring, and public outreach initiatives. Whether you've benefited from a natural viewshed by taking pictures of pristine landscapes, listened to the call of the loon, or found connection and comfort in the quiet and solace of the Adirondack Park—consider donating to these organizations to share your gratitude and help them continue their work.

Consider where you stay.

The Adirondack Park was founded with the idea of keeping it "forever wild." Stringent land use regulations arising from the state's commitment to preserving its natural resources mean that new development is challenging and housing inventory is low. While many people move to the region to retire or use their property as a second home, those who are or aspire to be full-time residents may find it difficult to buy a house. We recognize that the issue is complex, but we recommend making choices that support full-time local residents and the local economy when visiting.

Staying at locally owned hotels, motels, inns, and B&B's, as opposed to chains, is a great way to support local economies. Many motels and inns have been updated to feel more modern, provide keyless and check-in-free accommodations, and even provide amenities like lake beaches with fire pits and kayaks. If you are booking through services like Airbnb or VRBO, look to see if your host is a full-time resident and consider that perhaps your stay in their guest bedroom or guesthouse is funding their ability to live there year-round. You can also read their listing or bio to see what they are doing to support the community and environment around them, like maintaining a natural pesticide-free garden instead of a green lawn or offering composting for guests.

Buy local.

Shopping is a fun way to support the local economy *and* get the authentic feel of the Adirondacks. The region is known for its Adirondack furniture, birch-themed home decor, maple products, specialized outdoor gear, pack baskets, and craft beverages from various breweries and distilleries. Many of the more than one hundred small towns in the Adirondacks have businesses and boutiques that sell locally made or sourced materials, including Bolton Landing, Keene, Keene Valley,

150

HOW TO VISIT WELL

151

Lake George, Lake Placid, and Saranac Lake. Buy direct or visit one of the many local shops, markets, sugar shacks, and restaurants that carry their goods, wares, and harvests. By buying local, you're supporting local families and their livelihoods and businesses, and preserving the local culture and community that make this a special place. You're also lessening your environmental impact by reducing the carbon footprint inherent in transportation and shipping, and encouraging sustainable practices within the community.

Use only local firewood.

Forests are the Adirondacks' most beloved resource, and visitors can play a role in keeping them safe from invasive pests that kill trees, like the gypsy moth and the emerald ash borer. Avoid using untreated firewood from anywhere other than New York when visiting the region. If you need to, buy local firewood seen along most Adirondack roads.

Explore the low peaks, not just the High Peaks.

The Adirondacks are home to forty-six mountain peaks 4,000 feet in elevation or higher. Climbing them all has become a challenge and pastime of locals and visitors alike ever since the idea was introduced in the early 1920s by brothers Bob and George Marshall and their guide, Herbert Clark. Bob Marshall wrote about their experiences in his 1922 booklet *The High Peaks of the Adirondacks*. The booklet went on to inspire many more adventurers to follow in their footsteps, and since then more than seven thousand people have taken the challenge. When we asked locals their thoughts on how people can travel well in the Adirondacks, many of them confessed that while

EXPLORE THE ADIRONDACKS

they themselves were 46ers or saw the High Peaks as among the region's most distinguishable features, people ought to instead look around instead of *up*. There is so much *more* to enjoy and find on the trails, lakes, streams, and forests below the High Peaks.

Towns to Visit

The Adirondack Park differs from other large parks in that there are not just a few gateway towns but instead more than a hundred towns to explore throughout the region, each with its own character and lodging, dining, and recreation options. If you need time to recover from your wilderness adventures or simply want a small-town getaway with ample outdoor options, consider towns like Keene, Lake George, Lake Placid, Saranac Lake, and Tupper Lake.

Keene and **Keene Valley** are two charming, artsy hamlets packed with all the essentials—multiple bakeries, a coffeehouse, market, birch store, maple sugar farm, distillery, rustic furniture and goods store, and outdoor essentials store, The Mountaineer. Once you have all your gear, set out for a hike or climb from here, as you're surrounded by the Dix and Giant Mountain wilderness areas.

Lake George borders a lake beloved for its pristine and clear waters. This tourist town offers many options for shopping, dining, lodging, and getting out on the water. History lovers can ride a narrated historic steamboat and explore Fort William Henry, a museum that offers tours, field trips, and activities like military reenactments and interactive screenings of *The Last of the Mohicans*—a romanticized tale of the 1757 siege and surrender of Fort William Henry—which involve guides and reenactors marching and firing cannons and muskets along with the film. To get away from the crowds, **Bolton**

EXPLORE THE ADIRONDACKS

Landing is a nearby tiny town that offers lodging, dining, and shopping with the same access to the recreational opportunities that Lake George and the Schroon River offer—swimming, boating, and hiking. Be sure to stop by **Trees Adirondack Gifts and Books** for souvenirs and local literature.

Lake Placid hosted the Winter Olympics twice, in 1932 and 1980. This charming town in the heart of the Adirondacks is bopping year-round with a walkable main street offering many options for shopping, dining, lodging, and recreation. Sports fans and outdoor recreators rejoice—here you can ski Whiteface Mountain, visit the Olympic Center and the Lake Placid Olympic Museum, or visit where the "Miracle on Ice" took place.

Saranac Lake is a historic and picturesque small town, complete with a walkable downtown with coffee shops, a bookstore, restaurants, and boutique stores, and surrounded by lakes and mountains in every direction. Once a renowned destination for open-air treatment of tuberculosis, today it still offers the healing powers of fresh mountain air and natural beauty. Plus, a love for literature is apparent here at the Adirondack Center of Writing's storefront, not to mention the many literature-inspired traditions, events, and window displays throughout town—it's no wonder this town quickly became our favorite!

Tupper Lake is a tiny town with points of interest to explore like the Adirondack Sky Center and Observatory, and The Wild Center. This is one of those single gas station kinds of towns that makes you feel connected to a community but away from it all. Rest your weary feet while dining at the local brewery or restaurants that'll charm your socks off.

Where to Camp

Fish Creek Pond Campground, where most of the quiet and well-spaced campsites have water access. The waterfront campsites allow you to roll out of bed and go for a paddle or swim along pristine natural shorelines. In addition to boating, fishing, hiking, and swimming, this campground offers summer activities like crafts, games, and live entertainment at the amphitheater—making it a perfect destination for families.

Golden Beach Campground, for jaw-dropping lake scenery and sunset views. One of the most stunning campgrounds in the Adirondacks, this one in Raquette Lake offers large and well-forested campsites for privacy along with standard campground amenities.

Indian Lake Islands Campground, with boat access only. Paddle your way to island time on these beautifully wild, forested islands. Indian Lake offers endless opportunities for canoeing, boating, hiking, and fishing—and the campground offers picnic tables, fireplaces, pit toilets, and boat launches on Lewey and Indian Lakes.

Lewey Lake Campground, for a less primitive experience on Indian Lake that's accessible by land. This campground offers breathtaking views of the mountains and lakes along with amenities like clean bathrooms and showers.

Rogers Rock Campground, near Lake George. This family-friendly campground offers swimming, bicycling, fishing, boating, and hiking opportunities—in addition to group campsites.

Saranac Lake Islands Campground, with boat access only. Island camping is a quintessential Adirondacks escape-to-wilderness experience. The sites at this campground offer picnic tables, fire pits, and an outhouse. Catch your dinner en route to your campsite or along the shoreline of Saranac Lake.

In addition to these public campgrounds, you can also arrange campsites through camping companies, such as Hipcamp, that provide access to private land and campsites while supporting local communities and preserving natural spaces.

Community Resources

Adirondack Center for Loon Conservation (ACLC) is dedicated to inspiring a passion for and promoting the conservation of Adirondack loons. The ACLC conducts research on the Adirondack loon population, targeting environmental pollutants, factors affecting reproductive success, migration, health, and more—and collaborates with partners to use these scientific findings to influence policies for aquatic ecosystem protection. The organization also promotes environmental education and stewardship in classrooms and communities through exhibits, curricula, and field experiences. Visit the Adirondack Loon Center in Saranac Lake to see engaging exhibits and pick up some unique loon souvenirs.
adkloon.org

Adirondack Center for Writing (ACW) is a nonprofit with a mission to inspire the love of writing, reading, and storytelling. It does this through building and maintaining a community of writers, readers, and listeners; honoring the rich literary, cultural, and natural history of the Adirondacks; and partnering with diverse individuals, organizations, and schools to promote the craft of writing and the practice of reading in Adirondack communities. The center provides classes, workshops, readings, and other events for all ages, hosting some of the most widely attended and beloved events in the Adirondacks. These include the Kickass Writers Festival, the Howl Story Slam, the

158　　　EXPLORE THE ADIRONDACKS

Anne LaBastille Memorial Writers Residency and Women's Writing Weekend, and a creative writing workshop for teens. In addition to its storefront along the main street of Saranac Lake, which welcomes the public to come read and write, the center also engages the community through programs like Poem Village, an annual event where poems are hung on posters in store windows across the county, and installing a traveling Poetry Machine (a repurposed gumball machine) that dispenses free poems in local businesses. *adirondackcenterforwriting.org*

Adirondack Diversity Initiative (ADI) exists at the intersection of environmental and transformational justice. The ADI works to make the Adirondacks a welcoming and inclusive place for both residents and visitors while ensuring a vital and sustainable Adirondack Park for future generations. It focuses its efforts in five areas—education, commerce and economy, recreation, environmental justice, and public policy—through programming, outreach, mobilization, rapid response, and public policy efforts. *diversityadk.org*

Adirondack Experience, The Museum on Blue Mountain Lake (ADKX), preserves and interprets the diverse stories of Adirondack history, culture, and people to spark thoughtful dialogue and help shape the Adirondacks of the future. Formerly the Adirondack Museum, it has shared stories of the people who have lived, worked, and played in the Adirondack Park since 1957. The museum actively collects, preserves, and exhibits objects that were made or used by Adirondackers, along with photographs, books, collections of original manuscript materials, and works from painters, sculptors, and artisans inspired by the natural features of the Adirondacks.

COMMUNITY RESOURCES   159

It also houses a research library with the largest, most comprehensive repository of books, ephemera, manuscripts, maps, and government documents relating to the history of the Adirondack region—in addition to a makerspace where visitors can create their own inspired works.

theadkx.org

Adirondack 46ers is a nonprofit hiking and service club founded to protect the wilderness character of the High Peaks region and to lead volunteer efforts and programs aimed at maintaining the trails. The club's members have climbed the forty-six major peaks of the Adirondacks and are dedicated to environmental protection. They teach outdoor skills, pick up litter, steward the High Peaks trailheads and trails, mentor aspiring 46ers, give out scholarships, donate bear cannisters, provide educational materials, and support and partner with organizations with similar goals and initiatives in the Adirondacks.

adk46er.org

Adirondack Land Trust (ALT) is a private land-saving group that aims to forever conserve the forests, farmlands, waters, and wild places that advance the quality of life of Adirondack communities and the ecological integrity of the Adirondacks. Projects have included improving hiking access, supporting farmers and farming communities by protecting thousands of acres of agricultural lands through easements, creating stewardship endowments that fund perpetual care of farms and forests under conservation easements, creating preserves to protect landscapes and beloved viewsheds, establishing new state forests, and purchasing wild shoreline to protect water quality.

adirondacklandtrust.org

160   **EXPLORE THE ADIRONDACKS**

Adirondack Mountain Club (ADK) is a nonprofit that works to protect the wild lands and waters of New York state by promoting responsible outdoor recreation and developing a statewide land stewardship community. The ADK provides outdoor education through dozens of programs aimed at every level from outdoor novice to expert, and it manages the Adirondacks High Peaks Summit Stewardship Program. Since 1922, the organization has worked to increase access to the backcountry by building trails, conserving natural areas, and publishing definitive guidebooks and maps. The ADK's Cascade Welcome Center between Keene and Lake Placid provides information and recreation on its 12 miles of trails.
adk.org

Adirondack Mountain Reserve (AMR) is a private landholding in the Adirondack Park owned by the Ausable Club. This extremely popular destination is the gateway to nearly a dozen High Peaks and popular places like Indian Head and Rainbow Falls. The AMR is accessible to the public through a foot traffic easement but requires users to obtain a day-use permit to access the trails and follow a set of guidelines to preserve the natural environment and respect private property.
hikeamr.org

Six Nations Iroquois Cultural Center, owned by a Mohawk of Akwesasne family, is a place where the public can view more than three thousand artifacts illustrating the culture of the Haudenosaunee (Six Nations of the Iroquois) Confederacy. The center affirms traditional Native values, philosophies, and sensitivities through educational experiences for students as well as visitors to the Adirondack Park, and aims to help everyone better understand the history, culture, contemporary realities, and potential futures

COMMUNITY RESOURCES

of Native Nations. Listen to storytelling lectures and browse the gift shop, featuring Mohawk baskets, beadwork, books, T-shirts, silver jewelry, and acrylic paintings that reflect Six Nations culture. *6nicc.com*

The Wild Center is a 115-acre science-based center in Tupper Lake. The center offers experiences, exhibits, and programs designed to showcase the natural beauty and biodiversity of the Adirondack region while opening new ways to look at our relationship with nature. Through indoor and outdoor interactive exhibits, live animal displays, and educational programs highlighting the flora, fauna, and ecosystems of the Adirondacks, the center aims to ignite an enduring passion for the Adirondacks and inspire a future where people and nature thrive together. One of the highlights is a treetop walkway called the Wild Walk, where you can get an elevated view of the surrounding forest, explore a four-story twig tree house, swing on bridges, clamber over a spider's web, and climb to a full-size bald eagle's nest.
wildcenter.org

Essential Reads

A Year of Moons: Stories from the Adirondack Foothills
by Joseph Bruchac (Fulcrum, 2022)

In the Adirondacks: Dispatches from the Largest Park in the Lower 48
by Matt Dallos (Empire State Editions, 2023)

Legends of the Iroquois
by Tehanetorens, Ray Fadden (Native Voices, 1998)

Short Carries: Essays from Adirondack Life
by Elizabeth Folwell (Adirondack Life, 2009)

Adirondack Portraits: A Piece of Time
by Jeanne Robert Foster (Syracuse University Press, 1986)

The Blueline Anthology
edited by Rick Henry, Anthony O. Tyler, Stephanie Coyne-Deghett, Myra Gann, Alan Steinburg, and Alice Wolf Gilborn (Syracuse University Press, 2004)

ESSENTIAL READS

**The Adirondack Reader: Four Centuries
of Adirondack Writing, 3rd edition,**
edited by Paul Jamieson with Neal Burdick (Adirondack
Mountain Club, 2009)

**Braiding Sweetgrass: Indigenous Wisdom,
Scientific Knowledge, and the Teachings of Plants**
by Robin Wall Kimmerer (Milkweed Editions, 2013)

Woodswoman
by Anne LaBastille (Dutton, 1976)

Adventures in the Wilderness
by William H. H. Murray (Fields, Osgood, & Co., 1869;
Doublebit Press Legacy Edition, 2020)

The Healing Woods
by Martha Reben (Thomas Y. Crowell, 1952)

Acknowledgments

Working on this book series as parents to two young kids has required a village. Ilyssa, first and foremost, would like to thank Dave for supporting and encouraging her enthusiasm for this new *Campfire Stories* series and her decision to *not* plow right into a new job. With Ilyssa taking the lead on travel to research these books, Dave took on the primary responsibility for cooking every meal, doing every school or activity drop-off and pickup for two kids at two different schools, conducting the bedtime routine *every night,* and generally keeping our kids alive, full of snacks, and happy—often for a week at a time. Without Dave's unwavering belief in Ilyssa's passion and ideas, in addition to his editing and writing contributions, there would be no *Campfire Stories.* We'd also like to thank Ilyssa's mom, Diane Shapiro, who supports us during these times of travel and writing—and our many friends who host the girls for playdates and sleepovers.

Our daughters, Lula and Isla, also deserve thanks for inspiring us to pursue our passions and for their patience and understanding when we have to travel—even when it makes them feel like *a barnacle drifting all alone at sea.*

We are so grateful to Kate Rogers, editor-in-chief of Mountaineers Books, who curiously continues to entertain our *many* ideas, and—with honesty and great wisdom—helps to refine and shepherd them into the world. We extend this appreciation to the rest of the Mountaineers Books team, whose enthusiasm for our

ACKNOWLEDGMENTS

projects is deeply felt—and with a special shout-out to Joleen, who makes us feel like rock stars. To our editing team, Beth Jusino and Lorraine Anderson—we are grateful for your meticulous editorial work, and we admire your ability to take on a massive collection of stories spanning many centuries with enthusiasm and patience.

This series would not be what it is without Melissa McFeeeters, who has been with us from the very beginning and has designed all of our *Campfire Stories* projects—likely the reason you, reader, picked up our book in the first place!

We'd also like to thank the writers, librarians, researchers, and staff and/or volunteers of the many nonprofit organizations and museums we've connected with across the Adirondacks for your generosity and time. Our understanding of these places without your personal stories, lived experiences and history, and special connections to them would be far less authentic, passionate, and informed. We'd especially like to thank Betsy Folwell, who was more than generous with her time spent sharing her passion and deep, encyclopedic knowledge of the Adirondacks with us; Olivia Dwyer from the Adirondack Land Trust (and her team!) for the great insights and for sneaking us into the library when it was closed; and Jenny Ambrose, director of Archives and Special Collections at the Adirondack Experience, who went above and beyond identifying and pulling out source material and stories for us. We'd also like to thank Suzann Crumbok for being spontaneous and joining Ilyssa on this trip, keeping her company and laughing around campfires and throughout long drives.

To the bookstore buyers and staff who take time to chat with us while we're on our research trips, who educate us on local writers and important literature as well as carve a little space on your shelves for our book or feature it in your beautiful, creative displays—we see you and we appreciate you. We can't express how

ACKNOWLEDGMENTS

delighted we are to receive texts from friends and family traveling across the US who spot our books or card decks in the wild, or when we ourselves encounter them in real life. It never gets old.

Last, to our dear readers, whose insatiable desire for stories from our wild places allows us to continue collecting stories—we are grateful for your curiosity, love for our natural world, and desire to follow in the age-old tradition of storytelling. Without those readers who reached out or attended our events to say, *When are you going to do MY favorite place in the world?* or challenged us to consider places outside of national parks, we wouldn't have embarked on this new series.

Permissions and Sources

PERMISSIONS

Bachmann, P.H.W. "Adirondacks." *The Ad-i-Ron-Dac.* March–April 1949.

June Frankland Baker, "After Finding a Photo of Kensett's *Lake George, 1858,* in the Paper," in *The Blueline Anthology*, edited by Rick Henry, Anthony O. Tyler, Stephanie Coyne-DeGhett, Myra Gann, Alan Steinberg, and Alice Wolf Gilborn (Syracuse University Press © 2004). Reproduced with permission from the publisher.

Bruchac, Joseph. "Maple Sugar Moon" and "The Blanket Tree." Used by permission of Fulcrum Books.

Excerpt(s) from *In the Adirondacks: Dispatches from the Largest Park in the Lower 48* by Matt Dallos. Used by permission of Fordham University Press.

Fadden, David. "How the Birds Got Their Feathers." Printed with the permission of the author.

"Blinded by the Light" by Elizabeth Folwell was originally published in the August 2001 issue of *Adirondack Life* magazine.

PERMISSIONS AND SOURCES

Jeanne Robert Foster, *Adirondack Portraits: A Piece of Time*, edited by Noel Riedinger-Johnson (Syracuse University Press © 1986). Reproduced with permission from the publisher.

Kimmerer, Robin Wall. "Blue Line Medicine." Printed with the permission of the author.

Excerpt(s) from *Woodswomen: Living Alone in the Adirondack Wilderness* by Anne LaBastille, copyright © 1976 by Anne LaBastille. Used by permission of Dutton, an imprint of Penguin Publishing Group, a division of Penguin Random House LLC. All rights reserved.

Excerpts from Wandering Home by Bill McKibben. Copyright © 2005, 2014 by Bill McKibben. Reprinted by permission of St. Martin's Press. All Rights Reserved.

The editors have made every effort to locate all of the copyright holders for the excerpts included in this book. In some cases, however, they were unable to locate the appropriate person or entity or confirm the publication date or other relevant details. If anyone has information on any of the poems, stories, or essays included here, please contact the editors at hello@campfirestoriesbook.com.

SOURCES

"About the Haudenosaunee Confederacy." Haudenosaunee Confederacy, www.haudenosauneeconfederacy.com/who -we-are/.

Adirondack Regional Tourism Council, "Facts about Adirondack Black Bears." Visit Adirondacks, visitadirondacks.com/about /adirondack-animals/black-bears.

"Adirondacks: Native Americans." National Park Service, www.nps.gov/articles/adirondacks-native-americans.htm.

PERMISSIONS AND SOURCES

Bassett, Joyce. "Remembering Grace's Legacy." Adirondack Explorer, 10 March 2024, www.adirondackexplorer.org/stories/amazing-grace-hudowalski.

Clement, Michelle. "The Origin of the Great Camp Style Architecture." Adirondack Experience, 27 February 2015, www.adirondackexperience.com/story/2015/02/the-origin-of-the-great-camp-style-architecture.

"Common Loon Plumage and Body Structure." Loon Preservation Committee, loon.org/about-the-common-loon/appearance/.

"Eastern Cougars." Adirondack.Net, www.adirondack.net/wildlife/cougars/.

"Fred M. Rice." Historic Saranac Lake Wiki, localwiki.org/hsl/Fred_M._Rice.

"History of Fort William Henry." Fort William Henry Museum, www.fwhmuseum.com/history/.

"Loon Natural History." Adirondack Center for Loon Conservation, www.adkloon.org/loonnaturalhistory.

Morris, Chris. "#NFCT20: Back to Where It Started." Northern Forest Canoe Trail, 28 May 2020, www.northernforestcanoetrail.org/nfct20-back-to-where-it-started/.

Silber, Debra Judge. "The Feel-Good Recliner That Cures What Ails You." *Smithsonian Magazine*, 4 August 2021, www.smithsonianmag.com/innovation/how-adirondack-chair-became-feel-good-recliner-cures-what-ails-you-180978322/.

"Sucker Brook Preserve." Lake George Land Conservancy, lglc.org/preserves/sucker-brook-preserve/.

"Timbuctoo: African American History in the Adirondacks." Adirondack Experience, www.theadkx.org/timbuctoo-african-american-history-in-the-adirondacks/.

"Trail Overview." Northern Forest Canoe Trail, www.northernforestcanoetrail.org/discover/trail-overview/.

Vermillion, Stephanie. "See New England's Vibrant Fall Foliage on an Epic Canoe Trail." *National Geographic*, 28 September 2020, www.nationalgeographic.com/travel/article /paddle-the-longest-inland-water-trail.

"William Chapman White." Historic Saranac Lake Wiki, localwiki.org/hsl/William_Chapman_White.

Young, Terence. "The Minister Who Invented Camping in America." *Smithsonian Magazine*, 17 October 2017, www.smithsonianmag.com/history/religious-roots-of -americas-love-for-camping-180965280/.

Directory

NORTHERN ADIRONDACKS

Lyon Mountain Fire Tower
visitadirondacks.com/recreation/ hiking/fire-towers

Lyon Mountain Trail
Trailhead and parking lot on Lowenburg Rd, Lyon Mountain

HIGH PEAKS

High Peaks Information Center
adk.org/high-peaks -information-center
Mount Marcy via
Van Hoevenberg Trail
1002 Adirondack Loj Rd,
Lake Placid

South Meadow Farm
southmeadow.com
67 Sugarworks Way,
Lake Placid

KEENE AND KEENE VALLEY
townofkeeneny.com

Black Rooster Maple
blackroostermaple.com
10819 Route 9N, Keene

Cedar Run Bakery and Market
cedarrunbakery.com
2 Gristmill Ln, Keene

Old Mountain Coffee Company
oldmountaincoffee.com
1767 Route 73, Keene Valley

Rainbow Falls
ausableriver.org/explore /waterfalls/rainbow-falls-amr
Indian Head Trail, Adirondack
Mountain Reserve
Route 73 and Ausable Rd,
Keene Valley

The Mountaineer
mountaineer.com
1866 Route 73, Keene Valley

Valley Grocery Store
1815 Route 73, Keene Valley

NEWCOMB
newcombny.com

**Camp Santanoni
Historic Area**
*dec.ny.gov/places/camp
-santanoni-historic-area*
Gate Lodge Parking Area,
Newcomb Lake Rd,
off Route 28N

**Goodnow Mountain
Fire Tower**
*visitadirondacks.com
/recreation/hiking/fire-towers*
Goodnow Mountain Trail
*Trailhead and parking lot on
Route 28N*

WILMINGTON
townofwilmington.org

**Cloudsplitter Gondola
(at Whiteface)**
*whiteface.com/todo/cloudsplitter
-gondola-summer*
5021 Route 86

High Falls Gorge
highfallsgorge.com
4761 Route 86

**Whiteface Mountain
Veterans' Memorial Highway**
*whiteface.com/todo/whiteface
-veterans-memorial-highway*
Route 431

TRI LAKES

**Six Nations Iroquois
Cultural Center**
6nicc.com
1466 County Hwy 60, Onchiota

LAKE PLACID
lakeplacid.com

**John Brown Farm
State Historic Site**
*parks.ny.gov/historic-sites/29
/details.aspx*
115 John Brown Rd

The Bookstore Plus
thebookstoreplus.com
2491 Main St

SARANAC LAKE
saranaclake.com

**Adirondack
Center for Writing**
adirondackcenterforwriting.org
15 Broadway

Adirondack Loon Center
adkloon.org/adklooncenter
75 Main St

DIRECTORY

Bitters and Bones
bittersandbones.com
65 Broadway

Eagle Island Camp
eagleisland.org
442 Gilpin Bay Rd

St. Regis Canoe Area
dec.ny.gov/places/saint
-regis-canoe-area
Numerous parking areas
accessed from Route 30

White Pine Camp
whitepinecamp.com
White Pine Rd, Paul Smiths

TUPPER LAKE
tupperlake.com

Coney Mountain Trail
tupperlake.com/hiking/coney
-mountain
Trailhead and parking lot on
Route 30

Mount Arab Trail
tupperlake.com/hiking/
mount-arab
Trailhead and parking lot on
Mount Arab Rd, Piercefield

The Wild Center
wildcenter.org
45 Museum Dr

CHAMPLAIN VALLEY

lakechamplainregion.com

Ausable Chasm
ausablechasm.com
2144 US Route 9,
Ausable Chasm

Champlain Valley Trail
empiretrail.ny.gov
Empire State Trail from
Whitehall north to Keeseville
(on-road bicycle route)

Crown Point State Historic Site
parks.ny.gov/historic-sites
/crownpoint/details.aspx
21 Grandview Dr, Crown Point

Fort Ticonderoga
fortticonderoga.org
102 Fort Ti Rd, Ticonderoga

Lake Champlain Bikeways
champlainvalleynhp.org
/recreation/lake-champlain
-bikeways
Champlain Bikeway from
Crown Point north to Keeseville
(on-road bicycle route)

Lake Champlain Bridge
www.dot.ny.gov
/lakechamplainbridge
Bridge Rd, Crown Point

Lake Champlain Byway

lakechamplainbyway.com
In Vermont, US Route 7 through
Chittenden County and US
Route 2 through Grand Isle
County

North Star Underground Railroad Museum

northcountryunderground
railroad.com/museum.php
1131 Mace Chasm Rd,
Ausable Chasm

Poke-O-Moonshine Mountain Fire Tower

visitadirondacks.com/recreation
/hiking/fire-towers
Poke-O-Moonshine Mountain
Trail
176 US Route 9, Lewis

Sail Adirondacks

sailadks.com
54 Harbour Ln, Port Henry

CENTRAL ADIRONDACKS

Pharaoh Lake Wilderness

dec.ny.gov/places/
pharaoh-lake-wilderness
Numerous parking areas and
trailheads near the towns of
Schroon Lake, Ticonderoga,
Hague, and Horicon, with main
access via Routes 74, 8, and 9N

BLUE MOUNTAIN LAKE

adirondackexperience.com
/adirondack-towns/blue
-mountain-lake

Adirondack Experience

theadkx.org
The Museum on
Blue Mountain Lake
9097 Route 30

Blue Mountain Fire Tower

visitadirondacks.com/recreation/
hiking/fire-towers
Blue Mountain Trail
Trailhead and parking lot on
Route 30

Chef Darrell's Mountain Diner

bluemtdiner.com
8814 Route 30

The Hedges

thehedges.com
122 Hedges Road

INDIAN LAKE

indianlakeadk.com

OK Slip Falls

adirondackexperience.com
/hiking/ok-slip-falls
OK Slip Falls Trail
Trailhead and parking lot off of
Route 28

West Canada Lake Wilderness

dec.ny.gov/places/west-canada
-lake-wilderness
Numerous parking lots and trailheads near the towns of Indian Lake, Arietta, Lake Pleasant, Morehouse, and Ohio, with main access via Routes 30, 28, and 8

LONG LAKE AND RAQUETTE LAKE

mylonglake.com

Great Camp Sagamore

sagamore.org
1105 Sagamore Rd,
Raquette Lake

Lake Kora

lakekora.com
1185 Sagamore Rd,
Raquette Lake

Northern Forest Canoe Trail

northernforestcanoetrail.org
Western terminus on Route 28, Old Forge

Owl's Head Fire Tower

visitadirondacks.com/recreation /hiking/fire-towers
Owl's Head Mountain Trail
Trailhead and parking lot on Endion Road, Long Lake

The Waldheim

thewaldheim.com
502 Martin Rd, Eagle Bay

SOUTHERN ADIRONDACKS

BOLTON LANDING

Bolton Landing Brewing Company

boltonlandingbrewing.com
4933 Lake Shore Dr

Trees Adirondack Gifts and Books

4942 Lake Shore Dr

LAKE GEORGE

visitlakegeorge.com

Million Dollar Beach

dec.ny.gov/places/lake-george -beach-day-use-area
Lake George Beach
Day Use Area
139 Beach Rd

Prospect Mountain Veteran's Memorial Highway

Routes 9 and 9N

Shepard Park and Beach

lakegeorge.com/business /shepards-park-beach-8741/
Canada St

About the Contributors

Henry Abbott (1850–1943) was a jeweler, watchmaker, and author based in Manhattan and later New Jersey who is remembered for inventing and manufacturing the Calculagraph, a device to measure elapsed time. He was known as a raconteur, and between 1914 and 1932 he privately published his series of nineteen Birch Bark Books about camping, hunting, and fishing in the Adirondacks to hand out to friends.

Poet **June Frankland Baker** was born in Schenectady, New York, and graduated from SUNY Albany. She taught in North Syracuse and Skaneatels, New York, and Longmont, Colorado—and now resides in Washington state with her family.

Writer and storyteller **Joseph Bruchac** draws on his Abenaki roots in recounting traditional tales of the Adirondacks and the Northeastern Woodlands. He has authored more than 120 books for adults and children as well as poems, articles, and stories that have appeared in more than five hundred publications, including *National Geographic, Parabola,* and *Smithsonian Magazine.* Beyond his own published work, Bruchac has edited many anthologies that include writing from Asian American authors, Indigenous authors, and prisoners.

ABOUT THE CONTRIBUTORS

Matt Dallos is a PhD candidate at Cornell University, where he teaches environmental writing seminars. He lives in the Finger Lakes of New York.

David Fadden has a reputation for being a painter, but he is also a storyteller, illustrator, writer, and sculptor. His subjects range from traditional Haudenosaunee teachings to intimate and inspired portrayals of community members. David has exhibited his work throughout the northeast—including a solo show in 2020 at the Strand Center Gallery—and has partnered with the Wild Center in Tupper Lake, New York, the John Brown Farm Historic Site in Lake Placid, and Akwesasne Tourism. Much of his work can be seen at the Six Nations Iroquois Cultural Center in Onchiota, a facility founded in 1954 by his grandparents where he and his brother Donny continue to break down stereotypes and share accurate understandings of Mohawk and Haudenosaunee culture.

Elizabeth Folwell has lived and breathed all things Adirondack since she moved to Blue Mountain Lake in 1976. She was the education coordinator at what was then called the Adirondack Museum (now the Adirondack Experience), operated a general store in town along with her husband, directed the Adirondack Lakes Center for the Arts from 1980-1988, and served as editor and creative director of Adirondack Life until 2020. She is the author of Short Carries: Essays from Adirondack Life and the first three editions of The Adirondack Book, a local guidebook. She serves on the board of the Adirondack Land Trust and Friends of the Tuscarora Steamboat.

Jeanne Robert Foster (1879–1970) was born into poverty in the Adirondacks and went on to travel and live across the world in cities like New York City, Boston, London, and Paris where she became a fashion model, poet, literary editor, and journalist in the

180   ABOUT THE CONTRIBUTORS

1920s. Through her travels, Foster wrote and published articles and immersed herself in the international arts and cultural scene where she befriended famous writers and artists. Her poetry can be found in collections like *Neighbors of Yesterday*, *Wild Apples*, and a 1986 collection of her work *Adirondack Portraits: A Piece of Time*.

Robin Wall Kimmerer is a mother, scientist, writer, and SUNY Distinguished Teaching Professor at the SUNY College of Environmental Science and Forestry in Syracuse, New York, and also the founding director of the Center for Native Peoples and the Environment. Her writings include *Gathering Moss*, which was awarded the John Burroughs Medal for Nature Writing in 2005, and the best-selling *Braiding Sweetgrass: Indigenous Wisdom, Scientific Knowledge, and the Teachings of Plants*. In 2022, she was awarded a MacArthur Fellowship and elected to the National Academy of Sciences.

Anne LaBastille (1933–2011) was an Adirondack guide, writer, and ecologist, best known for her four-volume Woodswoman autobiography. Wanting to be close to nature, she built her own cabin on Twitchell Lake in the western Adirondacks, but she also traveled around the world as an environmental consultant, helping to document endangered species and create nature preserves. She wrote sixteen books, more than a hundred articles, and dozens of scientific papers, and served as a commissioner with the Adirondack Park Agency for nearly twenty years.

Bill McKibben is an environmentalist, journalist, and author of the bestselling book *The End of Nature*, considered to be the first book on climate change for a wide audience. Named "one of the world's 100 most important global thinkers," McKibben is the recipient of a Gandhi Peace Prize, holds honorary degrees from twenty universities and colleges, is a founder of the grassroots climate

ABOUT THE CONTRIBUTORS

campaign 350.org, and even has a new species of a woodland gnat named after him, *Megophthalmidia mckibbeni*.

Alan Steinberg (1944–2023) was a professor in the Department of English and Communication at SUNY Potsdam. He authored several books, including the short story collection *Divided*, the novel *Cry of the Leopard*, and the poetry collection *Fathering*, which won the Seventh Annual National Poetry Chapbook competition. Although he was born and raised in New York City, he came to love the rugged beauty and challenge of the North Country.

Alfred B. Street (1811–1881) was a writer and poet born in Poughkeepsie, New York. He practiced law before serving as New York state librarian for more than thirty years, and published books of verse and prose. Among the latter are *Woods and Waters, or the Saranacs and the Racket* (1860) and *Lake and Mountain; or, Autumn in the Adirondacks* (1870).

William H. H. Murray (1840–1904) was an American author, minister, and outdoorsman credited with popularizing the American outdoor movement in the late 19th century. Known as "Adirondack Murray" for his writings on the Adirondack Mountains, his 1869 book *Adventures in the Wilderness; or, Camp-Life in the Adirondacks* became a best-seller launching him into fame and sparking a surge of interest in wilderness recreation, outdoor adventures and leisure activities including camping, hiking and fishing.

William Chapman White (1903–1955) was a foreign correspondent in the early 1930s, a columnist for the *New York Times* and the *New York Herald Tribune*, and author of the 1954 book *Adirondack Country*, a history of the region.

About the Editors

Ilyssa Kyu is the founder of Amble, a sabbatical program for creative professionals to take time away with purpose in support of nature conservancies. She is a design researcher and strategist with a degree in industrial design and previously worked at boutique and global design studios. She is currently using her design consulting experience to support nature nonprofits through All Hands, a creative collective, as well as continually dreaming up ways to integrate her love for storytelling and the outdoors.

Dave Kyu is a socially engaged artist and writer. Born in Seoul, South Korea, and raised in the United States, he explores the creative tensions of identity, community, and public space in his work. He has managed public arts projects for the Asian Arts Initiative, Mural Arts, and the City of Philadelphia. His own creative projects have found him commissioning skywriting planes to write messages 10,000 feet above Philadelphia and doing everything Facebook told him to do for a month.

Together, they've created the *Campfire Stories* book and card deck series. They were artists-in-residence at Independence National Historical Park in Philadelphia, PA—a collaboration between the NEA, the National Park Service, and the Mural Arts Program—which resulted in an event, "I Will Hold You in the Light," which brought together six diverse performers responding to the theme of "The Pursuit of Happiness."

MORE CAMPFIRE STORIES

Campfire Stories bring together the beauty of the natural world and the traditions of storytelling across cultures in order to build deeper connections to our public lands.

Tales & Travel Companions:
The Adirondacks
Cape Cod
Chesapeake Bay
The Redwood Coast
The San Juan Islands
Santa Fe & Taos

Tales from National Parks and Trails:
Campfire Stories
Campfire Stories, Volume II

Cards to Ignite Imagination:
Campfire Stories Deck
Campfire Stories Deck for Kids!

recreation • lifestyle • conservation

MOUNTAINEERS BOOKS, including its two imprints, Skipstone and Braided River, is a leading publisher of quality outdoor recreation, sustainability, and conservation titles. As a 501(c)(3) nonprofit, we are committed to supporting the environmental and educational goals of our organization by providing expert information on human-powered adventure, sustainable practices at home and on the trail, and preservation of wilderness.

Our publications are made possible through the generosity of donors, and through sales of 700 titles on outdoor recreation, sustainable lifestyle, and conservation. To donate, purchase books, or learn more, visit us online:

MOUNTAINEERS BOOKS
1001 SW Klickitat Way, Suite 201 • Seattle, WA 98134
800-553-4453 • mbooks@mountaineersbooks.org
www.mountaineersbooks.org

An independent nonprofit publisher since 1960